COMMUNICATION ETHICS

ACTIVITIES FOR CRITICAL THINKING AND REFLECTION

Spoma Jovanovic

Tammy Swenson Lepper

Leeanne M. Bell McManus

Melba Vélez Ortiz

Robert L. Ballard

Michelle A. Leavitt

Lori Charron

Kendall Hunt
publishing company

www.kendallhunt.com
Send all inquiries to:
4050 Westmark Drive
Dubuque, IA 52004-1840

Copyright © 2021 by Kendall Hunt Publishing Company

ISBN: 978-1-7924-5358-8

Published in the United States of America

Dedication

To Kenneth Andersen and Roy V. Wood, for pointing us to the path and guiding us on the way.

contents

Acknowledgments

As a group, we acknowledge Veronica Lempert (B.A., Pepperdine University) for providing a student perspective and reminding us that while we may be the professors in the classroom, learning never ends for any of us. We remain students of communication and communication ethics. We express our appreciation as well to Dr. Stephen Bloch-Schulman whose unconventional ideas and creative thinking informed our own in writing this book. Finally, thank you to Paul Carty, Director of Publishing Partnerships, and Angela Willenbring, Senior Development Coordinator, for the opportunity to work with Kendall Hunt.

Robert (Bert) Ballard, Pepperdine University, Malibu, CA. *My gratitude and admiration go to the co-authors of this book who model communication ethics in their personal and professional lives, striving for ethics of responsibility and care, alongside their continued commitment to each other, wherever life takes us. I extend my life-giving acknowledgment to the many students who keep me sharp, and to Pepperdine University, who provided me freedom to continue this project. Finally, to my family—Sarah, Adria, Kyla, and Jayden—who gave up their time so this project could teach others about communication ethics.*

Leeanne M. Bell McManus, Stevenson University, Stevenson, MD. *I would like to thank my extraordinary colleagues for their unwavering commitment to this project. This group has encouraged and inspired me throughout this writing journey. Thank you to my students for allowing me to try new activities in the classroom. Thank you to my mentors, Ronald C. Arnett and Janie M. Harden Fritz. They have supported me and shared their wisdom throughout my academic career. Thank you to my family (Mark, Isabella, and Elouise) for enduring my crazy schedules and being my inspiration along the way.*

Lori Charron, St. Mary's University of Minnesota, Winona, MN. *This project has been a joy to work on with my "virtual department" coauthors. It is a privilege to work alongside such passionate and thoughtful experts as we pursue our passion in communication ethics. Our friendships are the best product of our work. Thank you to Dr. J. Vernon Jensen whose teaching and mentoring initiated my life-long academic journey. Thank you to my students at Saint Mary's University who encourage my love of teaching every day. A special thanks to Prof. Dean Beckman, Dr. Marilyn Reineck and Prof. Tasha Van Horn for providing consistent support and friendship. Finally, I am deeply grateful to my family. To my daughters, Kelsey and Julia, thank you for your editing skills, coffee trips, and younger generation perspectives. To my sisters, Gaye Lindfors and Julie Benedict, thank you for keeping tears of laughter fueling my work. To my husband, thank you for leaning a little harder into the yoke when I was working on this book—and for reminding me why I do what I do.*

Spoma Jovanovic, University of North Carolina-Greensboro, Greensboro, NC. *My deep appreciation goes to the co-authors of this book whose wisdom and talents demonstrate how education illuminates new paths to hope. I extend my thanks as well to treasured Communication Studies faculty* *colleagues and students in Greensboro who see ethics as a core value worth expressing in all we do. I remain grateful to the leadership and work of University of California's National Center for Free Speech and Civic Engagement for its support of expression and engagement in public life. Thank you, too, to my family, especially Lewis, Jay, Sander, and Lena who remind me that our commitment to one another is the basis of our profound expression of ethics.*

Michelle A. Leavitt, William Jessup University, San Jose Campus, San Jose, CA. *I am grateful to my co-authors whose commitment to communication ethics inspires me daily. Thank you to my students for their openness to learning about communication ethics through these activities. I am deeply grateful to my mentor and dissertation advisor, Dr. Roy V. Wood, for introducing me to the study of communication ethics and inspiring my journey to live out what we teach. I appreciate the steadfast support and encouragement of my parents, Mary Ann and Raymond Holly; husband, Glenn; and children, Madeline and Miles.*

Tammy Swenson Lepper, Winona State University, Winona, MN. *Thanks to all of the students who have taken ethics courses with me and been game for my sometimes outlandish activities and assignments. You inspire me to make my classes better every day. Thank you to my family (Todd, Hannah, and Rachel) for patiently putting up with my ongoing excitement about this book and its contents. My dissertation advisor, David Rarick, modeled what ethical collaboration looks like, for which I am eternally grateful. Thanks also to this group: my research family, my virtual department. I am so fortunate to know and work with you; your kindness, compassion, and collaboration are a guiding light.*

Melba Vélez Ortiz, Grand Valley State University, Allendale, MI. *Thank you to my master teacher Dr. Clifford G. Christians for shaping me as a communication ethics teacher. Thank you to my intellectual family Spoma Jovanovic, Leeanne Bell McManus, Lori Charron, Tammy Swenson-Lepper, Michelle Leavitt, Robert Ballard, and all of their loved ones for creating and sustaining the magic that led to this project. Thank you to my extended intellectual family at the Communication Ethics Division of the National Communication Association for its never-ending supply of inspiration and stimulus. Finally, many thanks to my dear friend Dr. Patrick D. Anderson, a blueprint of what a scholar is supposed to be and whose feedback enriched my contribution to this project.*

Robert L. Ballard (Ph.D., University of Denver) is the former Blanche E. Seaver Professor of Communication at Pepperdine University. He researches communication ethics and intercountry adoption. His work has appeared in *Encyclopedia of Communication Ethics, Sage Encyclopedia of Research Methods, Communication Education, International Review of Qualitative Research, Journal of Family Communication,* and *Qualitative Inquiry.* He is a former Chair of the Communication Ethics Division of the National Communication Association and was named Communication Ethics Teacher of the Year in 2015.

Leeanne M. Bell McManus (Ph.D., Duquesne University) is a Professor in the Department of Communication Studies at Stevenson University. She has co-authored three books, *Communication ethics literacy: Dialogue and difference, Conflict between persons: The origins of leadership* and *Event planning: Communicating theory and practice.* She is a past Chair of the National Communication Association's Communication Ethics Division and Past President of the Eastern Communication Association. She teaches and conducts research in communication ethics, conflict, and event planning.

Lori Charron (Ph.D., University of Minnesota) is a Professor of Business & Communication. Additionally, she is the department's Basic Course Director and Editorial Board member for *The Journal of Literacy and Technology* (JLT). Her academic interests include communication ethics, interpersonal communication (focusing on leadership), and communication pedagogy. Her most recent, lead author, publication is entitled, *Credo for Ethical Distance Learning,* published in JLT, 2020. Dr. Charron's vocational passion is making her academic interests relevant for her students.

Spoma Jovanovic (Ph.D., University of Denver) is a Professor in Communication Studies at the University of North Carolina, Greensboro. She collaborates on community initiatives with grassroots organizations to advance dialogue and creative action. A former Chair of the Communication Ethics Division of the National Communication Association, Jovanovic is author of *Democracy, Dialogue and Community Action: Truth and Reconciliation in Greensboro* (University of Arkansas) and a 2019-2020 Fellow with the University of California's National Center for Free Speech and Civic Engagement.

Michelle A. Leavitt (Ph.D., University of Denver) is a former Chair of the Communication Ethics Division of the National Communication Association and an Instructor at William Jessup University in San Jose, California. Her research interests include communication ethics, civil rights, and rhetoric. She has co-authored two publications, which appear in *Communication Education* and the *Journal of the Association for Communication Administration.*

Tammy Swenson Lepper (Ph.D., University of Minnesota) is a Professor and internship director in the Communication Studies Department at Winona State University. Her research interests include communication ethics, ethical sensitivity, pedagogy and communication ethics, organizational communication, and service learning. She is a former Chair of the Communication Ethics Division of the National Communication Association. Her most recent publication, for which she was lead author, "Cyberbullies, Trolls, and Stalkers: Students' Perceptions of Ethical Issues in Social Media," was published in the *Journal of Media Ethics.*

Melba Vélez Ortiz (Ph.D., University of Illinois at Urbana-Champaign) was born and raised in Puerto Rico and is a Professor of Communications in the Frederik Meijer Honors College at Grand Valley State University. She is a former Chair of the Communication Ethics Division of the National Communication Association. Her research interests include communication ethics, global ethics, intellectual history, and environmental communication. Her most recent publication *Maatian Ethics in a Communication Context* (Routledge Press, 2020) details how the classical ethical approach of *Ma'at* guided public communication practices in ancient Egypt.

These authors have a passion for teaching communication ethics and welcome questions, suggestions, and conversation around these activities. Reach out to them at communicationethics.activities@gmail.com

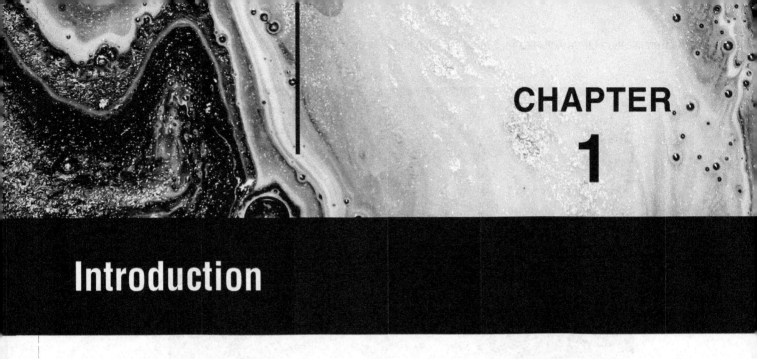

Introduction

Sarah, who's living in a first-year residence hall, knows that her friend Bekah from down the hall isn't doing very well. Bekah is depressed, anxious, and harming herself. Sarah worries her friend might be thinking of suicide. Bekah has asked her not to tell anyone about her mental health issues, but Sarah wonders if that's the right thing to do. Should she keep Bekah's secret? If so, for how long? If not, who should she tell and why? This situation may be scarily familiar to you. Do you keep a friend's secret and maintain your relationship, or do you tell someone who could help Bekah, and potentially end your friendship?

Many students who study communication encounter situations similar to the one involving Sarah and Bekah, which causes them to ask questions. What are the best ways to respond to difficult situations, or when is it right to speak up rather than remain silent? After my roommate abruptly walked away from our lease, what could I say and do to restore good relations with my landlord and my former roommate? If I become ill with a virus, what information is right to share, with whom, and in what ways? If a career opportunity arises for me to work for a public relations firm that represents a company harming the environment, what should I do? How can I address my public officials to get policies changed so our community will have more affordable housing? These are just some of the questions you will face as you enter your college years. Our goal in writing this book is to help you figure out how to make informed decisions about many of the ethical questions you will face throughout life. Our goal is not to tell you the answer, but to help aid you in making the best ethical decision. Many of our ethical decisions are not always clear and simple, but usually fall in the gray area, causing more questions. In this book, you will learn that communication ethics is less about rules—and even much less about clarity—than it is about discovery: learning what people in your community value and why, learning what **you** value and why, learning how the world ought to be different, and learning what you can do and how you can act to make it different.

Studying communication ethics requires asking questions, thinking about the possibilities, and reflecting on the consequences, rather than having answers handed to you. In fact, many times there isn't a single right answer. In addition, while the faculty who teach your class are experts in certain

ways, they don't have the final answers either. They are, more than anything, experts at knowing what questions to ask and helping you discover what information is needed to make an informed decision. They are experts at learning what knowledge is needed to make and communicate ethical decisions and helping you to learn where that knowledge might be found.

You may have taken a philosophy or business course on ethics where ethics was described as a way "in which one can raise a question about . . . [whether it] is *right* or *wrong*" (Neher & Sandin, 2007, p. 3). You might have read *Nicomachean Ethics* by Aristotle (1962), and discussed ethical dilemmas relating to public persuasion and good moral citizens. Even though *Nicomachean Ethics* is considered a primary book for the study of ethics, there are other perspectives on virtue ethics that emerged from thinking related to Confucianism, Taoism, Buddhism, Hindu Scriptures, Egyptian wisdom literature, 12th century Roman Christianity, Enlightenment thinkers, and even 18th century founders of American democracy (Ballard et al., 2016), just to name a few. All of these ideas might have been discussed in a traditional class on ethics and many of these ideas might already inform your decision-making. Unlike a traditional course on ethics, however, this book will situate the study of ethics within the field of communication. As a result, we will walk you through a short history of communication ethics to help you understand why the emphasis on *communication* ethics is important.

Short History of Communication Ethics

As a field of study, communication is seen as essential for every major. The National Communication Association (NCA) states, "Communication focuses on how people use messages to generate meanings within and across various contexts, and is the discipline that studies all forms, modes, media, and consequences of communication through humanistic, social scientific, and aesthetic inquiry" (NCA, n.d., para 1). Communication occurs in various contexts, including interpersonal, organizational, intercultural, and small groups, to name a few. As we start to think about all of these areas of communication, one common theme that emerges is that communication ethics permeates all forms of communication.

Communication ethics has been defined "as a process of reasoning aimed at providing sound justifications for or against particular communication behaviors, choices, messages, and acts" (Ballard et al., 2016, p. 155). Moreover, it is "the recognition that we take a given philosophy of communication, an understanding of the good, and apply it in interaction with others. The study of communication ethics is the study of philosophy of communication brought into engaged communicative application in the marketplace of ideas" (Arnett et al., 2018, p. 30). As you think of definitions of communication ethics, what does that mean to you? As you deepen your understanding through study, critical thinking, and reflection, we imagine your definition of communication ethics may change. To define communication ethics, let's start by breaking down the phrase into its parts.

© maradon 333/Shutterstock.com

Defining Communication Ethics

How do you define communication?

_____

_____

_____

How do you define ethics?

_____

_____

_____

Now that you've defined *communication* and *ethics*, what is your starting definition of communication ethics? In other words, what connects communication and ethics?

_____

_____

_____

As you start to think about your own definition of communication ethics, consider how the study of communication ethics developed in the field of Communication Studies. Over the past 50 plus years, many scholars have grappled with understanding how ethics should be highlighted within the field of communication. By reading this book, you will have a better understanding of how communication and ethics are inseparable.

From the early 1980s until the present we have seen a substantial increase in the study of communication ethics. In 1983, a prominent scholar in communication ethics, Kenneth Andersen, declared the theme of the then Speech Communication Association (now National Communication Association) *Communication Ethics and Values*. Andersen encouraged communication scholars to recognize the ethical implication for communication and engage communication ethics within their scholarship. The convention's focus on ethics led to Andersen's presidential address entitled *A Code of Ethics for Speech Communication*, proclaiming communication ethics as an essential component to the discipline of communication. As a result of his address, a Communication Ethics Division was created within the NCA and a biannual conference devoted to communication ethics was established (Andersen, 2000). Years later, Andersen (2005) was invited by NCA to give The Carroll C. Arnold Distinguished Lecture that he titled *Recovering the Civic Culture: The Imperative of Ethical Communication* to reiterate the importance of communication ethics.

To further recognize the importance of communication ethics, NCA approved a *Credo for Ethical Communication*. This credo or statement of beliefs discusses the importance of ethics to communication processes and says, "Ethical communication is fundamental to responsible thinking, decision-making, and the development of relationships and communities within and across contexts, cultures, and media" (NCA, 1999)[1]. This credo is used as a guiding reference to establish criteria for ethical communication. If you are a member of the communication honor society, Lambda Pi Eta (LPH), you follow the guidelines set by the NCA Credo for Ethical Communication. There are many other organizations that provide codes of conduct. You might belong to the Public Relations Student Society of America (PRSSA) or participate in the National Student Advertising Competition hosted by the American Advertising Federation (AAF), each has standards for professional behavior. An ethical credo acts as a starting point for appropriate conduct. Your initial class activity will be to establish a credo of ethics standards based on codes, procedures, and standards of communication ethics.

The goal of this book is to help you unpack, discover, and recognize the importance of becoming an ethical communicator in a diverse world. In light of this, we want to give you an overview of how each of the dozens of activities in the book is designed and formatted for clarity. The activities revolve around four main areas of inquiry or questions, related to your **knowledge**, **skills**, **values**, and **action**.

1. Questions to expand **knowledge** focus on what you need to know to be ethical in the society you live in today and how you can learn these things. Answering these questions includes researching who already knows what you need to know (for instance, experts, activists, or government officials). It means asking, what is it that they know and how can you learn what you need to know?

2. Questions about **skills** ask you to consider what skills do you need to develop—or further develop—to understand your ethical responsibilities and how to live up to them. Answering these questions includes identifying the skills you already use and defining what other skills you will need. It also means asking who has the skills that you need and how can you learn from them? In this area, you may also reflect on why a particular skill is more important to learn than others—because time is limited, and you cannot learn everything. Skills in this category might include formal decision-making processes or strategies you can use to write a code of ethics or an ethical post for social media.

3. Questions related to **values** investigate what others value and why, and ask you to identify what you value and why. Answering these questions means recognizing that, while you may say you know what you value, when tested, pushed, and invited to think hard and talk with those who have different views, you may find that you have not considered other things that you value as well. Or, you might find you better understand why you value what you do.

4. Questions about **action** focus on what you should do or what actions you should take. Here, we also invite you to consider how you can communicate in ways consistent with your own values while continuing to learn from others. Answering these questions means learning from others how they live by their values, what opportunities are there for you to live by your values, and what that looks like. Actions might include speaking up when you hear someone say something you think is unethical, or it may mean attending a protest, or taking political action.

---

[1] The language of the Credo is intentionally non-academic and non-technical in order to pass "the airplane test"—that the Credo could be shared with and understood by someone you meet on an airplane (Anderson 2000, p. 140).

In working through the activities and assignments in this book, you will not find universal answers and you may not even find one right answer to refer to throughout the semester. Instead, you will be guided to engage in critical thinking and reflection, which are needed so that the actions you take in your life communicate a thoughtful consideration of the relevant people, issues, and perspectives. This section includes three additional activities to begin this process, including the *Developing a Code of Ethics*, *The Check In*, and *Communication Ethics and Abilities*.

Chapter Activities

Developing a Code of Ethics

You and your classmates will write a code of ethics for your class to help guide your own, your peers', and your professor's communication behavior throughout the semester. Having a standard to refer to will help your group communicate more ethically and provide you with a safe space to learn how to offer and receive suggestions about how to communicate more ethically.

The Check In

This activity provides an opportunity for you to share some personal information about yourself and to get to know your classmates better. Done regularly, it becomes a practice or ritual that promotes community, equality, safety, trust, and open communication.

Communication Ethics and Abilities

Have you ever been curious what it would be like to navigate your campus or community as someone with a disability might? This activity gives you the opportunity to explore familiar spaces with a new perspective and to consider the ethical implications of accessibility or the lack of it.

Developing a Code of Ethics

During your first-year college orientation or your first day on a new job, you were probably given some type of written code of conduct. These rules and regulations allow you to figure out what is defined as acceptable and unacceptable behavior. Unfortunately, many of us toss these rules aside without taking the time to review and reflect on the guidelines that will be used to evaluate our conduct. This activity will allow you and your classmates to create a credo of communication ethics for your class. Your goal will be to actively engage your class credo to allow for thoughtful discussion based on critical thinking and reflection.

In this activity, you'll increase your *knowledge* by thinking about:

- What is appropriate classroom conduct?
- Does appropriate classroom conduct change when discussing controversial topics? What rules are already in place for you to follow?

You'll have the opportunity to learn *skills* by considering:

- What guidelines or behaviors can you follow that promote ethical communication in the classroom?

You can consider your own *values* and that of others by asking:

- What ethical values drive conversation in the classroom?
- Do some ethical values suppress conversation/encourage conversation?

Putting what you learn into *action* means asking:

- How do you engage in ethical conversation in the classroom?
- How do you and others communicate both verbally and nonverbally to be an ethical communicator?

The Activity

1. Organize yourselves into small groups.

2. Review the NCA Credo for Ethical Communication (NCA, 1999), below:

NCA Credo for Ethical Communication
(approved by the NCA Legislative Council, November 1999)

Questions of right and wrong arise whenever people communicate. Ethical communication is fundamental to responsible thinking, decision making, and the development of relationships and communities within and across contexts, cultures, channels, and media. Moreover, ethical communication enhances human worth and dignity by fostering truthfulness, fairness, responsibility, personal integrity, and respect for self and others. We believe that unethical communication threatens the quality of all communication and consequently the well-being of individuals and the society in which we live. Therefore we, the members of the National Communication Association, endorse and are committed to practicing the following principles of ethical communication:

We advocate truthfulness, accuracy, honesty, and reason as essential to the integrity of communication.

We endorse freedom of expression, diversity of perspective, and tolerance of dissent to achieve the informed and responsible decision making fundamental to a civil society.

We strive to understand and respect other communicators before evaluating and responding to their messages.

We promote access to communication resources and opportunities as necessary to fulfill human potential and contribute to the well-being of families, communities, and society.

We promote communication climates of caring and mutual understanding that respect the unique needs and characteristics of individual communicators.

We condemn communication that degrades individuals and humanity through distortion, intimidation, coercion, and violence, and through the expression of intolerance and hatred.

We are committed to the courageous expression of personal convictions in pursuit of fairness and justice.

We advocate sharing information, opinions, and feelings when facing significant choices while also respecting privacy and confidentiality.

We accept responsibility for the short-and long-term consequences for our own communication and expect the same of others.

- Review your course syllabus.
- Find and review any other documents related to classroom conduct, like your university's conduct code.

Once you have reviewed the various documents that offer guidelines for rules and regulations in the classroom, create your own Credo for Ethical Classroom Communication.

Create five guidelines that encourage civil communication in the classroom.

1. Respect others opinions

2. Challenge

3. Accountability

4. Application of ideas outside of class

5. Incorporate personality and Humor

Write a three-sentence rationale for why these points are important.

Next, create some talking points to share with your class. You will be given 3 to 5 minutes to discuss with your fellow classmates what your group created. Incorporating ideas from each group, create a credo for your class. Copy your final class credo in the box below:

As conversations get difficult in the classroom, please refer to this credo created by the class to allow for open and honest communication.

Discussion Questions

1. What new information did you learn from creating the class's credo? What did you learn about your instructor's course policies? Your college or university's conduct code? What did you learn about communication ethics?

2. What encourages you to add to class discussion or what causes you to be silent? What skills do you use to encourage others to speak?

3. Does the credo for ethical classroom communication conflict with any of your personal values? If so, how or in what ways? How can you ethically express disagreements you may have with the class's credo? Are any of your values about communication not represented in this code? If so, what's missing? How important is it for you that those values are included? What action can you take to include those values in your class's code?

4. How can you continue to enforce the credo for ethical communication throughout the semester? How can you incorporate what you learned from creating this code into your everyday life? In what situations are you likely to think about and apply this code?

References

Andersen, K. E. (2000). Development in communication ethics: The ethics commission, code of professional responsibilities, code for ethical communication. *Journal of the Association for Communication Administration, 29,* 131–144.

Andersen, K. E. (2005). *The Carroll C. Arnold Distinguished Lecture 2003: Recovering the Civic Culture: The imperative of ethical communication.* Pearson Education.

Aristotle. (1962). *Nicomachean ethics* (M. Ostwald, Trans.). Bobbs-Merrill.

Arnett, R. C., Fritz, J. M. H., & Bell, L. M. (2018). *Communication ethics literacy: Dialogue & difference* (2nd ed.). Kendall Hunt.

Ballard, R. L., Hoffer, M., & Bell McManus, L. M. (2016). Communication ethics: A vital resource in an ever-changing world. *Choice: Current Reviews for Academic Libraries, 54,* 155–164.

National Communication Association (NCA). (1999). *Credo for ethical communication.* Retrieved January 22, 2020, from https://www.natcom.org/advocacy-public-engagement/public-policy/public-statements

National Communication Association. (n.d.). *Definition of communication.* https://www.natcom.org/about-nca/what-communication

Neher, W. W., & Sandin, P. J. (2007). *Communicating ethically: Character, duties, consequences and relationships.* Allyn and Bacon.

The Check In

This activity provides an opportunity for you to share some personal information about yourself and to get to know your classmates better. Done regularly, it becomes a practice or ritual that promotes community, equality, safety, trust, and open communication. Feminist ethics likewise recognize the importance of acknowledging the whole person by operating from a platform of care in which learning can best occur (Noddings, 2013).

With this activity, you'll increase your *knowledge* by considering:

- What influences how people manage their day-to-day obligations?

You'll have the opportunity to learn *skills* by asking:

- What are the ways to listen attentively and openly?
- What is appropriate information to share with a large group, when, and why?

You can consider your own *values* and that of others by asking:

- What ethical concerns and perspectives emerge as relevant to someone's well-being?
- Are there ways you can express care through listening, talking, and other behaviors to strengthen your community?

Putting what you learn into *action* means considering:

- How can you use and modify *The Check In* with other groups and for what purpose?
- In what ways is your class session better (or not) because of *The Check In*?

The Activity

The point of *The Check In* is to be honest with your classmates and to be able to acknowledge and thereby set aside other concerns, thoughts, and issues that could interfere with your full participation in class. How much you disclose about yourself is up to you, always. Respond briefly to one of the following prompts:

1. Who do you turn to when you have an ethical question and why that person?
2. What concerns, fears, or worries are you holding?
3. What is a piece of advice you have received that has helped you?

Reference

Noddings, N. (2013). *Caring: A relational approach to ethics and moral education* (2nd ed). University of California Press.

Communication Ethics and Abilities

Beyond Empathy, Experiential Brushes with Privilege

Dr. Peggy McIntosh is the former associate director of the Wellesley Centers for Women at Wellesley College in Massachusetts. Her approach to the study of social privilege is rooted in the women's studies research tradition and has been invaluable to the scholarship on disabilities. In 1989, she published "White Privilege: Unpacking the Invisible Knapsack," a scholarly article that brought issues of privilege into discussions of oppression. Though her invisible knapsack was originally applied to the problems of racial inequality, the approach has been used since that time to illuminate a range of social issues including those pertaining to ability.

McIntosh's method consists of listing items in the knapsack of privilege, meaning unearned and invisible privilege that white people (or in this case able-bodied people) unconsciously carry throughout their lives. By unearned McIntosh means that a thing was given to us by the accident of birth, such as one's physical features. By invisible privilege she means the kinds of opportunities, choices, expectations, and rewards to which an individual has access. Alternatively, it also refers to the kinds of things the color of your skin (or in this case physical abilities) free you from having to worry or care about. For example, many people do not have to think about the weight of a bathroom door but people managing physical challenges might. By engaging this method, we do not want to make able-bodied people feel guilty or bad about themselves or even promote empathy toward the struggles of those who have visible or invisible disabilities. The goal, following the invisible knapsack method, is to help you reflect on your own advantages by providing you with an opportunity to briefly experience the world stripped of some of those privileges.

Communication ethics scholars have engaged issues of disability in a variety of contexts including stereotyping (Christians et al., 2020), listening and discursive practices (Parks, 2018), and rhetorical interruptions (Hyde & Rufo, 2000), among many others. Today is your day to go beyond theorizing

© SeventyFour/Shutterstock.com

to engage in application. What will you learn about yourself? How might the experience gained through this activity improve your ability to communicate ethically?

In this activity, you'll increase your *knowledge* by experiencing and asking:

- How does the campus look to people with disabilities?
- What does it feel like to navigate campus with a limited range of choices?

You'll have the opportunity to learn *skills* by considering:

- What many advantages or disadvantages do you face daily as a result of your particular set of abilities?
- How might your lived experience in this activity improve your ability to communicate ethically about disabilities?

You can consider your own *values* and that of others by asking:

- What issues, obstacles, or difficulties does your particular set of abilities spare you from worrying about? Or, conversely, force you to think about?
- In what ways does the privilege of being able-bodied confer a person advantages when navigating campus?

Putting what you learn into *action* means asking:

- How can I use my experience in this activity to be a better, more ethical communicator?
- What have I learned in this exercise that I can use to advocate for others?

The Activity

This activity requires at least 75 minutes and can be done in a face-to-face setting or remotely. If done on campus, the activity can be modified for social distancing and masks. Your instructor will direct you toward Option 1a or 1b.

1a. Visit all of your classes, but only use handicap entrances, elevators, and curb ramps (i.e., you may not step up curbs or use stairs). Try to start by finding each handicap parking area, then proceed to your classroom using only elevators and curb ramps (no stairs). Also, use only handicap entrances (or at least find them and then enter using a regular door). Pay special attention to whether there are hills on your campus, think about the ways you might need to get from point A to point B if you were on crutches or in a wheelchair or had some other physical challenge. Again, find the handicap parking outside the building before you start and use (or identify) the handicap entrances.

Use the same protocol for visiting six campus locations/offices such as:

- The campus library
- The office of the President of your college/university
- The campus bookstore

- The counseling office
- Student employment office
- The campus disability resource office

If the office you are visiting is closed when you get there, it is acceptable to go to the office entrance and take a picture of the door to record your visit. After all visits are completed, answer the questions posed earlier to increase your knowledge, learn skills, consider values, and take action.

1b. Alternatively, you may choose to conduct this activity in your community. Only use handicap entrances, elevators, and curb ramps (i.e., you may not step up curbs or use stairs). Try to start by finding each handicap parking area, then proceed into the building using only elevators and curb ramps (no stairs). Also, use only handicap entrances (or at least find them and then enter using a regular door). Pay attention to whether there are hills, think about the ways you might need to get from point A to point B if you were on crutches or in a wheelchair or had some other physical challenge. Again, find the handicap parking outside the building before you start and use (or identify) the handicap entrances.

- Grocery store
- Gas station
- Department of Motor Vehicles
- Hospital
- Restaurant
- Fast food
- Park

2. Finally, using the data you gathered from the experience, create a short report answering the critical reflection questions below. Be sure to bring your report to class on the designated date for discussion.

- Before this exercise, had you noticed where all of the handicap accessible entrances, parking, and elevators were located?
- Were you able to complete this activity in the time allotted? If you were permanently or temporarily disabled, in what ways would you have to adjust your schedule or day in order to arrive at your classes on time or visit the offices listed above?
- How did (or did not) the physical location of the Office of Student Affairs and/or other student-focused offices support students with disabilities?
- What grade would you assign your college/university (A-F) for its accessibility if you were giving it a grade? What advice would you give to a prospective student with a disability about to attend your college/university? Would you recommend he/she/they attend? How does this exercise reveal your able-bodied privilege or able-bodied marginalization?

References

Christians, C. G., Fackler, M., Richardson, K. B., Kreshel, P. J., & Woods, R. H. (2020). *Media ethics: Cases and moral reasoning* (9th ed.). Routledge.

Hyde, M. J., & Rufo, K. (2000). The call of conscience, rhetorical interruptions, and the euthanasia controversy. *Journal of Applied Communication Research, 28*(1), 1–23. https://doi.org/10.1080/00909880009365551

McIntosh, P. (1988). White privilege and male privilege: A personal account of coming to see correspondence through work in women's studies. Wellesley College Center for Research on Women. https://www.racialequitytools.org/resourcefiles/mcintosh.pdf

McIntosh, P. (2012). Reflections and future directions for privilege studies. *Journal of Social Issues, 68*(1), 194–206. https://doi.org/10.1111/j.1540-4560.2011.01744.x

Parks, E. S. (2018). *The ethics of listening: Creating space for sustainable dialogue.* Lexington Books.

Additional Resources

Anderson, D., & Jones, B. (2019, November 19). Clinical psychologists debunk 25 of the most common myths about mental health and therapy. *Business Insider.* Includes video; relevant information starts at 17:09. https://www.businessinsider.com/depression-myths-schizophrenia-mental-health-debunked-25-2019-11

Grasgreen, A. (2014, April 4). Dropping the ball on disabilities. *Inside Higher Ed.* https://www.insidehighered.com/news/2014/04/02/students-disabilities-frustrated-ignorance-and-lack-services

Murphy, E. D. (2011, November 27). Post-traumatic stress disorder leaves scars 'on the inside,' Iraq veteran says. *Portland Press Herald.* https://www.pressherald.com/2011/11/27/post-traumatic-stress-disorder-leaves-scars-on-the-inside-iraq-veteran-says_2011-11-27/

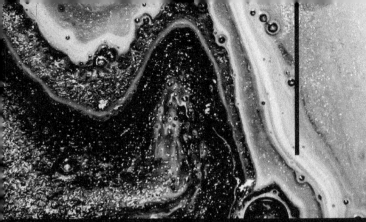

Ethical Perspectives and Philosophical Thinking

In many of your communication classes, we are sure you've learned about theory, or "any systematic summary about the nature of the communication process" (Dainton & Zelley, 2019, p. 7). Theories are important to understanding communication as they provide a basis from which to ask questions about what we observe about ourselves and others from a communication standpoint in a systematic way. For example, you might want to know more about *why* we choose certain media (Snapchat v. Instagram v. Hulu) over others and what needs (like escape, information, relaxation, social interaction, etc.) the media meet for us. To best answer these questions, you might draw on Uses and Gratifications Theory by Elihu Katz (see Griffin et al., 2018), which offers an explanation for why people seek out certain kinds of media in order to satisfy particular needs. Questions from theory are usually research-focused that ask about cause and effect or that seek to gain deeper

© Viacheslav Lopatin/Shutterstock.com

This illustration titled *The School of Athens*, by Italian painter Raphael, dates to the European renaissance period (1511) and is significant in its rare depiction of the vital role Islamic scholars and women played in the rediscovery, translation, and popularization of Ancient Greek philosophy. The painting offers a more accurate depiction of philosophy and ethics as the product of sustained dialogue between cultures and genders.

The painting features Hypatia of Alexandria, Egypt (370 AD–415 AD) a pioneer in the study of mathematics, astronomy, and philosophy. Raphael's painting also includes Averroes (1126–1198). Born in Córdoba, Spain, Averroes represents the pivotal role Muslim scholars played in the middle ages by translating and writing commentaries of the work of Aristotle and every other major ancient Greek thinker, who by the European middle ages had been forgotten.

understanding about communication behavior, which is exactly what you're asking when you wonder why we choose certain media to meet certain needs!

But when we are talking about communication ethics, we are asking different kinds of questions. While the questions still relate to communication behavior, rather than asking why, what caused something, or to more deeply understand some phenomenon we observe in ourselves or others, we are asking questions about values, impact, and if one *ought* to engage in a particular kind of communication behavior. Communication ethics helps us understand "how, in the absence of a universal ethical perspective in today's world, we can best coexist amid sometimes incommensurable differences" through "a system or process of reasoning in order to provide sound justification for or against particular communication behaviors, choices, messages, and acts" (Ballard et al., 2016, p. 1).

Broadly, communication ethics compels us to ask, "How ought I to respond?" When asking questions related to communication ethics, however, we do not employ theories but rather *perspectives*. If theories are asking questions about knowledge, perspectives orient us to ask questions about *values* and what we perceive to be *good* in any given situation. As Arnett et al., (2018) explain, "the good is the valued center of a given communication ethic—what is most important and … find[s] protection and promotion in our communicative practices" (p. 3). Said differently, communication ethics tries to identify and then promote a particular good or value.

But there are many different kinds of goods in the world and many goods may contradict each other. For instance, if you have a conflict with your roommate, it might be good to confront your roommate or it might be good to just not bring it up at all. How do we know what good is better in a situation like this? That's where perspectives come in. Perspectives are the basis from which to understand what is perceived as good.

Perspectives allow us to look at the same communication phenomenon with different points of view and with attention to the good that is being promoted and produced. It is important to understand this because when seeking answers to communication ethics questions, it often takes multiple points of view in order to arrive at a well–thought-out answer and reason. It is also important to understand that, unlike theory where you are often seeking one main answer, you may be using multiple perspectives and multiple points of view in order to better understand, reason, and justify yours and others' communication choices. In other words, you might have competing goods, but communication ethics lies in justifying the choices among those competing goods rather than trying to find a perfect answer. This requires some *philosophical thinking*.

Philosophical Thinking

Philosophy?! I'm in communication! I don't want to do philosophy! If you're thinking this and wondering why you are reading about philosophy and having philosophical discussions in your ethics class, you're not alone. But philosophical thinking is important. And while it is hard, it is actually very important for developing good communication skills. With a little effort and practice, like reading this book and completing the activities contained in it, it becomes a habit.

Ethics is actually one of the main five branches of the discipline of philosophy. The word philosophy itself comes from the Greek words *philo*, meaning lover, and *sophia* or wisdom, so the term *philosophy* is translated as lover of wisdom. The other four branches of philosophy also try to understand the human experience. *Metaphysics* (ancient Greek for beyond the physical) deals with questions related to all that informs human experience but lies outside of it, such as the concepts of space and time or even spirituality. *Epistemology* deals with questions of "how do we know what we know?" or "what credible evidence can count as true?" In other words, epistemology seeks to understand the standard for credibility and sense of truth. *Logic* is concerned with the ability to reason through, communicate, and express our claims to truth. For instance, investigating the structure and strength of arguments, types of arguments, and logical fallacies fall in the branch of logic. Finally, *aesthetics* deals with the nature and principles of beauty to better understand culturally specific or even universal standards of beauty and art.

That was a lot in one paragraph, and we do not expect you to fully understand it all after the first read through. People spend a lifetime studying these questions and ideas. But here's what you need to take away: The idea of loving wisdom (philosophy) involves studying aspects of human experience that are influenced by things beyond the human experience (metaphysics); what we consider to be legitimate ways of investigating truths (epistemology); proper reasoning techniques (logic); and principles and standards of taste and beauty (aesthetics). Ethics fits into this by helping us understand and respond to how humans promote the good and navigate what a culture considers its sense of right and wrong. The study and practice of ethics helps us (even you!) regulate individual and collective behavior based on free choice and decision-making. In other words, ethics deals with our ability to make and keep voluntary promises, our criteria for judging moral culpability or absolution, and the desirability of our own and others' values.

Here's the good news: Ethics is the branch of philosophy that engages theory and practice in equal parts. Ethics is guided practice and for that reason students of communication ethics need to hone their skills of appreciating and distinguishing between multiple ways of conceiving goodness and importantly strive to manifest communicative choices in practice, understanding the outcomes and consequences of communication behavior on ourselves and others. So, if you act without understanding ethics—philosophical thinking—the result may be impulsive, rash, counter-productive, or hurtful communicative behavior, no matter whether you intend it or not.

There are a few more things to consider in terms of philosophical thinking beyond understanding how ethics fits in with the rest of becoming a lover of wisdom (a philosopher). They include culture, ontology, inclusion, and consistency. We briefly review those next.

Culture

The study of communication ethics requires that we take an interest in the material and historical contexts that give rise to common sense assumptions about the nature of the good and the desirable. Take for example the culture that produced the ancient African ethic of *Maat*. *Maat* is born out of a society transitioning in the bronze age (3000 to 1200 BC) from nomadic groups to a unified agricultural society around 3100 BC. At its peak, ancient Egypt (Kemet as Egyptians then called their land) housed and fed anywhere from 1 to 1.5 million inhabitants. As an ethic, *Maat* promotes harmony, justice, and balance. It promotes kind speech, peace, and a strict adherence to the social order. Knowing the kind of historical and cultural period in which *Maat* originated and developed gives us an insight into why values and behaviors such as obedience to the social order, respectful speech, and listening skills were so important to ancient Egyptians and Africans. After all, these practices would have been essential to a continent dealing for the first time with large populations that began to share one location and resources.

Whether exploring Maatian or other ethical perspectives, ethics reflect a specific place and time in history. Ultimately, gaining an appreciation of the cultural roots of ethical theories can help you consider whether a particular set of ideas still has relevance to contemporary society or if, alternatively, historical and cultural conditions have changed sufficiently to warrant revision or rejection of any given view. From an ethical point of view, differing perspectives on ethics are neither truer (i.e., more right) nor more valuable than another. As ethical practitioners and investigators, you will learn to understand that the criteria by which to judge ethicality depend in large part on the applicable cultural worldview and historical moment in question. Thus, the study of foundational perspectives to ethics affords us a valuable window into the specific set of concerns, and to the often brilliant ways ethicists across time and place are able to articulate views in persuasive ways.

Ontology

Ontology is a part of metaphysics that studies the nature of being. In other words, it studies existence from a human standpoint—what it means to exist and how we as humans experience and make sense of that. Through ontological inquiry we gain an appreciation of the many and interesting ways various thinkers over time and place have defined for their communities what it means to be a good and decent human being. Almost invariably, each ethical perspective is grounded in its own ontology, or what it means to be human. Take Aristotle (a Greek philosopher who lived 382 to 323 BCE), who wrote about human beings as speaking animals, highlighting our unique and privileged ability to communicate through language. As a result, Aristotle built an ethical perspective that presumes speech as unique to humans and places emphasis on the responsibility all humans have to regulate and manage their communication and their behavior for the sake of the common good. Others, like Immanuel Kant (an 18th century Prussian philosopher), ground the essence of our humanity in our ability to reason. Consequently, Kant offers a standard for ethics and ethical behavior based on codes, norms, and duties to help keep humans oriented to the good. Meanwhile others, like Emmanuel Levinas (a 20th century French philosopher) believe humans to be full of hope, willing to risk that we will care for each other rather than commit violence against each other.

In sum, we can only issue ethical recommendations for how to achieve the common good (ethics) when we have identified what it means to be a person. If one thinks of the common good as that which benefits the most people, then ethicists need to clarify what it is they think we are (our ontology) before they can talk about what would benefit all or most of us. Thus, there is a deliberate interrogation of the nature of being embedded in every ethical perspective.

Inclusion

There are as many ways of understanding rightness and wrongness as there are people. An individual's values, beliefs, and commitments result from a unique personal history that includes, but is not limited to, the influence of parents, relatives, teachers, mentors, friends, culture, religion, and involuntary membership into social groups (i.e., gender, ethnicity). Similarly, ethical perspectives vary greatly in terms of focus and prioritization schemes. The Spaniard philosopher José Ortega y Gasset (1914/2000) famously described the nature of being as "I am I, plus my circumstance" and it is in this way that moral agents can generally be understood to be shaped by their social environments while retaining some degree of agency.

As a student of communication ethics, when you take an interest in the values that influence various ethical perspectives, you discover a wide and diverse collection of cultural concerns and worldviews that solidify over time into a distinct ethical perspective. The recognition that there is such an array of views on what is good, on a global scale and across time, may be disconcerting at first, but it reveals a key aspect of the human condition that makes dialogue an ethical necessity. Therefore, the study of foundational ethical perspectives provides a useful, *inclusive* lens to explore the many different ways the common good is conceptualized.

To assume that your own cultural values are superior to all others is itself a moral transgression that we call *ethnocentrism*. Though most of us begin life believing our culture makes more sense than others, an effective and ethical communicator understands that our culture is just one of many different ways to conceive of living rightly. Ethical communicators are committed to their values, while understanding others will likely hold their own in equal status. Thus, recognizing a multiplicity of ideas and making room for understanding different conceptions of the good do not require a relativistic stance on morality (that anything goes), but rather puts the onus on moral agents, organizations, and societies to address those differences through communication. Finally, inclusion itself can at times function as a protonorm or guiding principle for a given ethic. In today's day and age, communication ethics can lead us to inclusion that allows for difference, divergence, and disagreement while pursuing a common, yet diverse, good for all of us.

Consistency

Finally, investigating philosophical foundations of ancient and contemporary ethical perspectives sheds light into the importance of consistency to ethical practice. A major difference between ethics and law is that while laws are imposed on individuals by society (they predate one's birth and continue after one's death), ethics comes from within each person. In other words, there is no such thing as an ethical action that one was forced or coerced into. In this way often following the law is deemed ethical, but sometimes it is not. In most ethical frameworks, actions can only be judged to be ethical or not if the moral agent in question could have chosen to do otherwise. Noncoerced choice and decision-making are central to ethics and communication ethics. In critiquing one's own ethics or those of others, we must examine whether a moral agent's actions match the agent's stated commitments, one time or persistently. In this way, one's ethical character is built on the consistency with which our stated values are manifested through actions.

What's Next?

This introduction may feel a little overwhelming. That's okay. Most introductions are. The biggest thing to remember is that communication ethics works with perspectives, not theories, and communication ethics uses multiple perspectives at any given time in seeking answers to "How ought I to respond?" as it seeks the good to be promoted and produced. In order to be an effective communicator as well as a student and practitioner of communication ethics, engaging and learning philosophical thinking is important. It is also important to remain mindful and aware of the influences of culture, ontology, inclusion, and consistency when it comes to understanding ethics and ethical perspectives. We do not expect you to become expert philosophers, but some philosophical thinking is necessary. This section of the book now turns to reviewing six Western ethical perspectives: virtue ethics, duty ethics, consequentialist ethics, dialogic ethics, feminist ethics, and media ethics.

Virtue Ethics

Do you recall in elementary school when the principal or teacher would say something like, "Character counts!" and then list off a bunch of values like trustworthiness, respect, responsibility, fairness, caring, and citizenship (Character Counts!, 2020). Maybe it wasn't these values specifically, but in many schools, there were posters talking about different values and how to treat each other. You didn't know it then, but the school was trying to instill certain *virtues* in you and your classmates. Virtues are qualities that are deemed inherently good. Indeed, virtues and virtue ethics are commonly associated with 4th century BCE Greek philosopher Aristotle and *Nicomachean Ethics*, although there are also connections with Chinese Confucianism, Taoism, Buddhism, Hindu scriptures, Egyptian wisdom literature, 12th century Roman Christianity, Enlightenment thinkers, and the 18th century founders of American democracy. Recent work in virtue ethics by Alisdair MacIntyre (2007) has focused on practical action or *phronesis*, while Martha Nussbaum (2013) has written on compassion in the civic and public sphere.

Aristotle's particular interest was the concern about how to best use speech to persuade others on public issues. In this way, the formal study of communication is often credited to Aristotle, and in this way speaking to persuade and ethics are also closely related. Virtues relate to both individuals and communities. Aristotle describes how a virtue is an expression of character formed through a habit to the extent that the more we engage in expressing that virtue, the more our character reflects that almost automatically. Virtue ethics is a personal, human activity rather than a creed, principle, or goal.

So how does this work in actual behavior? Let's pretend you caught your roommate cheating on a test. Although your roommate's act might not get caught by the teacher and it doesn't have anything to do with you, you have a dilemma: do you confront your roommate, do you bring it to the attention of the professor who you know and respect, or do you ignore it since it won't hurt anyone? A virtue ethics perspective challenges us to ask ourselves, *What kind of person do I want to be?* Or, what kind of character do I want to exhibit? What kind of virtues do I want to express? If you confront your roommate, you might be expressing courage. If you tell the professor, you might be expressing integrity. If you avoid, you might be expressing neutrality. It all depends. And that it depends is the crux of communication ethics: the question is *how ought I to respond?* while also being able to justify your choice. So, *what kind of person do you want to be?*

Duty Ethics

In the world of online learning that we all experienced during COVID-19, one of your instructors might have asked you to take a test and said the rules required you to not use your notes, books, or the internet. But if you used them, your professor would never know. At that point you had a decision to make: your professor would never know, but the rules stated you were not allowed to use outside sources. So, did you follow the rule or not? Did you lie?

These kinds of ethical questions relate to what are called duty ethics. Sometimes called deontological ethics, derived from the Greek *deon*, this perspective suggests ethical behavior is based on rules and reason. Immanuel Kant, who lived in the 18th century, is most often connected to this perspective that requires the same ethical response to a situation, no matter the circumstances. In *Foundations for a Metaphysics of Morals*, Kant says our ethical behavior is based on duties and moral obligations to a universal law that transcends human activity, which thus makes his view distinct from virtue ethics. One of the most famous of Kant's ideas is that of the *categorical imperative* in which a person acts based on principles that she/he/they would want everyone else to follow in *all* situations. The other main idea or maxim for which Kant is known is that we should never treat people as a means to an end, but always as an end in and of themselves. These formulations are nonnegotiable regardless of the person, situation, or outcomes; they should never be changed or modified. They are absolute, making ethics a *duty* to follow these principles.

So, let's get back to your online test situation. A duty ethics perspective would challenge us to ask, *What is the right thing to do?* Here, right has a special meaning; right means right no matter the circumstances, outcomes, situations, feelings, or relationships. What is *right* according to the categorical imperative? That is, what is *right* universally for all people, everywhere, and in all situations. For Kant, lying makes no reasonable, rational, or logical sense. For him, as he explains in *On a Supposed Right to Lie*, a lie anywhere destroys credibility, trust, and truth. Therefore, you should not lie at all, ever, at any time, and so in this case you should follow the rule to not use outside sources, no matter the consequence (like if you fail) or if you will get caught or not.

Duty ethics can be hard because it feels like we do not have a choice, and in a lot of ways this is accurate if you strictly follow Kant's conceptualization. Think, for instance, of someone hiding a friend who will get arrested if found, yet the friend is innocent. For Kant, lying to authorities about the friend's whereabouts, would be unethical. The circumstances simply don't matter.

However, we rely on duty ethics frequently. For instance, if you always write up end of shift summaries at your workplace, you are engaging in duty ethics. If you are religious and you attend worship or prayer services regularly, you are engaging in duty ethics. Married couples express their love in words and deeds as a duty to commitment. If you always respond to texts from your parents, you are expressing a duty to respond. Subject these to Kant, then they might fail the categorical imperative if taken to the extreme and you might end up in a lot of logic games and circular reasoning with no end or feel like you don't have a choice. For Kant, choice from an ethical perspective meant, do I do my duty or not? And if I do not, then I am not really using my choice-making abilities very well. This is the opposite of virtue ethics, which says that your choices determine your character.

But we do apply duty ethics constantly in our day-to-day lives when we choose to do what is right regardless of the consequences, situations, feelings, or relationships. When you choose to do the right thing, you are applying a duty ethics perspective. Duty ethics, like the other perspectives, is challenging. Here are some shortcuts when trying to decide if duty ethics applies. If the words rules, principles, or rights are mentioned, practically every time duty ethics will apply. Indeed, the Bill of Rights, the first 10 amendments to the U.S. Constitution, is all about certain universal, inalienable principles that are believed to be inviolable and apply to all people, all the time, everywhere.

As Lisbeth Lipari (2009) writes, duty ethics can be religious (e.g., The Ten Commandments), claim natural/inherent rights (e.g., United Nations Universal Declaration of Human Rights), or form the basis for social-contract theories (Jean-Jacques Rousseau). Other philosophers have developed rights-based approaches (e.g., John Rawls's theory of justice), discourse-based approaches (e.g., Jürgen Habermas's discourse ethics), and contract-based approaches (e.g., Thomas Scanlon's contractualism). Significantly for communication, both Habermas' and Rawls' theories center on processes of communication from which ethical norms and principles are derived. For more on these theories, see William Neher and Paul Sandin's (2017) book, *Communicating Ethically*.

Consequentialist Ethics

If virtue ethics centers on character and duty ethics centers on rules and rights, a consequentialist ethics perspective has to do with outcomes of choices, actions, and behaviors. Sometimes consequentialist ethics are called utilitarianism. Utilitarianism emerged from the thinking of 18th century British philosophers John Stuart Mill and Jeremy Bentham, who suggested that ethical decisions are made based on how they maximize happiness and benefit for the majority of people. This perspective is both quantitative (greatest good for the greatest number) and qualitative (promote happiness and avoid pain).

Of the three perspectives that we've looked at so far, this one often makes the most intuitive sense to us. For instance, if you choose to skip class and sleep in, we might first ask what the consequences of your action would be. Would you miss out on something important? Would it hurt you in class or an upcoming test? Would you miss out on seeing a friend? Do you need sleep more than you need the class lesson that day? You might ask these and many other questions in a split second as you lay in bed deciding whether or not to attend class.

However, beyond our everyday process of consequentialist ethics, utilitarianism asks us to use reason and to broaden our concerns of consequences and impacts beyond just ourselves. That is, utilitarianism asks us to consider others, both quantitatively (how many will benefit?) and qualitatively (how happy will they be?).

Policy decisions are often made using utilitarianism. For example, if we lower the tax rate, would it benefit a majority of Americans (number) with benefits and pleasure (more money in their paychecks)? Or, if we spend more on the military than education, would it benefit a majority of Americans in terms of security and happiness? These are not easy questions because the *impact* of these decisions is enormous. How can anyone or any group of people accurately predict how many people will be positively impacted by a decision, either in terms of numbers or overall happiness? In this way, utilitarianism is speculative and asks us to take risks with an uncertain future. A consequentialist ethics perspective challenges us to ask, *What is the impact of my actions on others?*

But let's return to whether or not you go to class. At first, it might seem like skipping class doesn't have that much to do with others, but that's not true. If you skip, your friend won't be able to see you. Your professor, who has put a lot of work, into preparing the lesson will feel undervalued. Your parents might feel less than appreciated if they are paying for your tuition. Your roommate might be frustrated as she/he/they were expecting to have the morning to practice a dance recital to loud music. Your classmates might miss out on an insight you could provide for them to better understand the lesson and in turn do better on an upcoming test. In short, there are many ways your choice to sleep in and skip class could impact others. Granted, these reasons, on balance, may not seem that strong or might be overly speculative. But the point is that a consequentialist ethics perspective challenges us to consider impacts on others.

Recent thinkers like Peter Singer (2015) have broadened this approach to include animals and the planet, asking, for instance, to what extent should we consider the impact of our actions on animals and the earth? In contrast to thinking beyond the human world to other forms of life, another form of consequentialist ethics is ethical egoism, which suggests that individuals ought to act solely according to rational self-interest because doing so provides psychological, emotional, evolutionary, and societal benefits. This perspective was popularized by Ayn Rand (1957/1992) to promote the value of wealth production in *Atlas Shrugged*.

Dialogic Ethics

Virtue, duty, and consequentialist ethics perspectives together form the foundation of classical ethics study. In most ethics classes you may take, whether it is in communication or other discipline, you will learn about these. From a communication ethics standpoint, they originate in philosophy and are applied to communicative actions, orienting us to the good of character, of rights and rules, and of impacts and consequences.

One of the most significant contributions of communication ethics to these foundational perspectives is dialogic ethics, which locates ethics in the communicative relationships between people. In short, it asks what ought to be our response and responsibility to *the other* and what happens between you and the other.

Let's return to the scenario where you caught your roommate cheating on a test. If you used a virtue ethics perspective, you are concerned with your character and the kind of person you want to be; if you used a duty ethics perspective, you are concerned with what is right, which is to confront your roommate regardless of your relationship or circumstances; and if you used a consequentialist ethics perspective, you are concerned with the impacts on others overall, like if cheating will impact the curve. But a dialogic ethics perspective challenges us to ask, *How do I value and include the other?*

Everyone has a narrative and perspective, because in narratives we are making sense of our world and our lives. It is a way we bring an understandable order to our lives and how we engage the world beyond us. Your roommate who was cheating on a test has a story—an ordered reason—for why she/he/they cheated. In dialogic ethics, your roommate is offered an opportunity to share her/his/their reasons for cheating in a space that is, at least initially, neutral and nonjudging.

Listening, taking the other seriously, and valuing the other before yourself are touchstones of dialogic ethics. In dialogic ethics, we seek first to understand the other, no matter how strange, absurd, or even unethical it might seem at first glance, before we seek to be understood. A shorthand for this might be: listen first, speak second. Further, dialogic ethics creates a process and space for the other to be heard. It takes the other seriously on the other's terms.

Communication scholars often point to 20th century Jewish philosophers Martin Buber and Emmanuel Levinas as the ones who introduced dialogic ethics. Buber (1970) emphasized mutuality and reciprocity, suggesting that we relate to others along a continuum of *I-It* to *I-Thou*. In an I-It relationship, typically we do not reveal much of ourselves to the others, and we treat another as indistinguishable from the many others, thereby keeping ourselves somewhat distant from each other. In contrast, an I-Thou relationship is one of mutual vulnerability, where trust, authenticity, and intimacy emerge. Levinas' (1985) focus was somewhat different, directed instead on our responsibility to and for others in communication. Levinas did not think reciprocity among people was desirable, and instead urged that we be *response-able* for others in the world who are infinitely different than ourselves. Levinas called this difference between us, radical alterity. In this way, ethics is putting the other before and above the self without expectation of benefit in return. Rob Anderson, Leslie Baxter, and Kenneth Cissna (2004), along with Ronald Arnett (1986) and Michael Hyde (2001), have studied dialogic ethics to consider how communication constitutes and creates meaning, values, identities, relationships, cultures, and groups; others, like Spoma Jovanovic (2008), have viewed dialogic ethics as an underpinning for engaging in thoughtful community action. Dialogic ethics emphasizes openness to, interdependency with, and the inherent value of others.

So, you observed your roommate cheating on a test? It was, to you at first, clearly a violation of the instructor's policies. Rather than rush to a judgment, however, and express concern about the rules and principles (duty ethics), the impacts (consequentialist ethics), or your own character (virtue ethics), dialogic ethics would seek to understand why your roommate was cheating. Your first action might be to ask your roommate why she/he/they cheated. Your second action would be to listen without interruption, allowing your roommate to explain his/her/their decisions, reasons, and choices. Your third action would be to either ask questions or to tactfully offer your opinion and perspective. The key to dialogic ethics is not just a process, but also the hope that whoever is involved in the dialogue is *transformed* and influenced by each other because understanding is the goal.

It is important to understand that dialogic ethics itself does not render ethical judgment on the behavior *per se*, but the ethics orient us to the *inclusiveness* of all voices involved while cultivating a process and space whereby *understanding* and maybe even *transformation* can occur through a *mutual* sharing of exchanges and viewpoints. In the case of your roommate who cheated, by listening you may find that your roommate was unaware of the rules or the roommate is at the breaking point in terms of stress, grades, and family pressure. It is clear the roommate violated the policies, but a deeper understanding of your roommate may lead you to a different kind of response—maybe offering education on the policies or recommending a mental health counselor—rather than simply judging your roommate as immediately unethical and wrong.

Feminist Ethics

Let's face it, the history of the world is dominated by men and male voices. We're not judging—we're stating a fact. All of the previous perspectives originated in the minds of men—Aristotle with Virtue Ethics, Kant with Duty Ethics, Bentham and Mill with Consequentialist Ethics, Buber and Levinas with Dialogic Ethics. And while these have provided the world important and necessary ideas and contributions related to ethics and morality, their unintended consequence is that women's voices and ideas have largely been ignored and silenced.

In the 1970s, along came Carol Gilligan. Gilligan recognized this historical silencing and the oppression of women's voices, ideas, and status. This required a feminist-based alternative to ethics. Specifically, in response to the leading moral theory of development at the time by psychology professor Lawrence Kohlberg (1976), based on an ethics of justice, Gilligan (1982) offered an *ethics of care*. Further, Kohlberg's research was based solely on research with boys! Gilligan's alternative was based on women's experiences and psychological development. Both Gilligan and Kohlberg offer developmental, stage models.

For Gilligan, and other feminist ethicists, women and men are viewed as inherently equal, but due to sexism, women and men are socialized differently in ways that men's understanding and being in the world are the norm while women are viewed as secondary or exceptions (i.e., outside the norm) to men. The following table helps illustrate the differences between Kohlberg's and Gilligan's approaches.

		Kohlberg's Stages of Moral Development	Gilligan's Stages of Moral Development
Approximate Age Range	Stage	Goal/Substages	Goal
Birth to 9 years	Preconventional	1. Avoid punishment 2. Gain reward	1. Individual Survival
9 to 20 years	Conventional	3. Gain approval and avoid disapproval 4. Duty & guilt	2. Self-sacrifice is goodness
20+ years or maybe never	Postconventional	5. Agree upon societal rights 6. Universal principles/ personal moral standards	3. Principle of nonviolence – do not hurt self or others
		Ethic of Justice	***Ethic of Care***

Kohlberg's stages, based on an *ethic of justice*, emerged from Kant's duty ethics. Justice, here, is justice for all and not meted out differently according to different circumstances. Gilligan, on the other hand, aims to develop an ethics of care, one embedded within the network of human relationships where not hurting self or others is the primary good.

What does this mean in a real-life situation? Let's say you have to break up with someone. The relationship is one where you are not as into the other person as the other person is into you. There is nothing wrong with either of you, you just do not feel the same way as the other person. There is a more and less ethical way to break up. Kohlberg would challenge you to ask questions similar to duty ethics, *What is the right thing to do?* To answer, you would end up in a thought exercise about how if someone was unhappy, but the other person was happy, it's not an equal relationship and that could not hold in all circumstances universally. Gilligan, on the other hand, would challenge you to ask, *How can I demonstrate care and minimize harm for self and others?* With Gilligan, it is no longer about a universal principle or what might be right; instead, it is about ensuring that all parties feel cared for and that harm is minimized. At this point, you might use a process similar to dialogic ethics for explaining your different reasons and perceptions for the status of the relationship. Of course, at least one person will likely feel some harm, but having a conversation about feelings and perceptions that seeks to cultivate care is less harmful than explaining that it is your right to break up because there are unequal benefits. In this example and in all relationships, it is good and ethical to address problems directly rather than let inequities persist. Ethics can help orient you both to *how* to go about it as well as *what* may happen in this situation, including the harm that might occur.

It is important to understand that feminist ethics is not seeking to get rid of other ethical perspectives or even to replace them. Rather, it is offering an alternative perspective that seeks to take historically marginalized voices more seriously. Feminist ethics is not monolithic or singular; there are many different views and approaches within feminist ethics. Others doing work in this area include Seyla Benhabib (1992), Nel Noddings (2013), Rita Manning (1992), and Virginia Held (1995). bell hooks

(2014) has done a lot of work at the intersections of nonwhite and feminist perspectives. Feminist ethics has helped pave the way for other nondominant perspectives including indigenous cultures, nonwhite, LGBTQ1, and economically impoverished. While there are many views and approaches, they share a commitment to political engagement and equality of all, both individually and systemically.

Media Ethics

If you followed any news coverage of the 2020 United States' Presidential election, you were aware that some news channels may have portrayed some candidates more positively than others depending on the political party. Some channels may have given more airtime to some than others, or they may have shown more favorable images of some candidates than others. And, when you watch news beyond the United States, like the BBC or Al-Jazeera, they bring their own cultural lenses and influences to their news coverage of our election process, sometimes critical and sometimes amusing. Yes, we know that at times news channels sensationalize to get ratings, but even if we get beyond that, how do we decide which one is right in their reporting? Which one do we listen to? Which one is the most credible? The most ethical? This can be frustrating.

Media ethics tries to help us sort through misinformation. It emerged out of journalistic practices, seeking to understand what were the most ethical approaches to reporting news. It has grown into an important and influential branch of ethical thinking in the communication and journalism disciplines. Its overall orientation is to try to understand how media outlets (especially news media) influence the human condition along with striving to offer ethical guidance on media choices, including form, style, substance, and content.

Clifford G. Christians is the foremost media ethics scholar and theorist who often collaborates with others to advance research and thinking in this important field (Christians et al., 2020). He offers what he calls a communitarian approach, or better termed as communal or *communitas*. In this view, humans are first embedded in a community, within a fabric and network of human relationships. Media is an important connector and influencer in this network, maintaining, cultivating, and even destroying those relationships. Christians suggests, like many other media ethicists including Michael Traber (Christians & Traber, 1997), Patrick Plaisance (2018), and Stephen Ward (2011), that it is important to first recognize the networks of connections and *communitas* that we as humans are embedded in and approach them with justice, compassion, and stewardship. With *communitas*, there is a shift away from the classical approaches of virtue, duty, and consequentialist ethics that are preoccupied with individual rights and choices and a move toward a more pluralistic, communal, relational approach that is mediated by, well, media. Media ethics challenges us, then, to ask, *In what ways does this media influence the human condition and community?*

If we return to our news viewing, we might ask, then, how does one news channel's coverage of the election influence the human condition? Does it help us be more informed? Does it help us become better citizens? Does it encourage us to participate in the election process? Or, does it make us feel angry or to dislike others with different points of view? Does it make us feel more stressed and overwhelmed rather than better informed? Does it make us feel cynical toward participating in the democratic process? Even further, is this bias, or this slant, an appropriate use of media? If not, what would be better?

These are big questions without easy answers and with many different opinions. One process developed within media ethics to help work through these questions is the Potter Box (by Ralph B. Potter of the Harvard Divinity School). The Potter Box is a four-stage process depicted below:

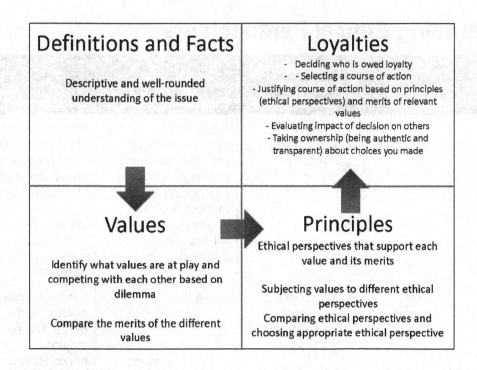

The first box (definitions and facts) is a description of the definitions and facts of the situation; the second box (values) is an identification of the competing values and their merits; the third box (principles) suggests an identification, analysis, and comparison of different ethical perspectives, and the fourth box (loyalties) relates to making the choice, justifying, and taking ownership. You might apply this by describing why coverage is biased (definitions and facts), the importance of critical thinking and sensationalism (values), the differences between duty ethics, consequentialist ethics, and feminist ethics (principles), and then selecting, say National Public Radio (NPR), because you believe their objectivity is more important than sensationalism (loyalties). The more you work with the Potter Box, the more you can address the two questions of media ethics: *In what ways does this media influence the human condition and community? And what is the appropriate way to use this media?*

Finally, media ethics also extols the need for professional codes of ethics. Again, while much more on this is in the field of journalism (see https://www.spj.org/ethicscode.asp), other media fields like advertising and public relations also have professional codes of ethics. Media ethics is necessarily broad, but work in this area focuses less on the media and more on the human and how media influences the human condition. Yet, the media has a profound influence on who we are, not just individually but socially and in *communitas* with one another.

Now that you have learned about ethics and some ethical perspectives, what follows is a chart illustrating the different perspectives covered and activities to put your learning into practice. Like all philosophical approaches, ethical perspectives become popular at different times in history and in varied cultural and religious contexts. Ethical perspectives tend to reflect the reigning values of the cultures of which they are born. The perspectives included in this chart, while foundational to the study of ethics in the West, are not exhaustive.

Understanding Ethical Perspectives

	Origins	Popularizing Figure and Famous Text	Evaluative Criteria	Criticisms
Virtue Ethics	Ancient Athens (4th Century B.C.E)	Aristotle, *Nicomachean Ethics*	Good character is the measure of virtue, practiced for example in being truthful, courageous, and modest. A person of good character will make good judgments.	What we value or consider as virtues changes over time and among cultures. Our values and virtues may conflict with one another. The impact of our actions is not considered, only the intentions.
Duty Ethics	Prussia, Germany (1780s)	Immanuel Kant, *Groundwork to the Metaphysics of Morals*	Categorical imperative: "Act on that maxim which you can at the same time will to be universal law." This means you have a duty to use reason and follow the rules so that you act the same way consistently, no matter the circumstances. Duty ethics views others, not as a means to an end, but as an end in itself.	It is never okay to lie or cheat in this view of ethics. The standard may be too rigid, not considering the situation, or the impact of relationships, and emotions in decision making. Having universal rules is impractical.
Consequentialist Ethics	England (1860s)	John Stewart Mill and Jeremy Bentham, *Utilitarianism*	Maximizing principle: "The greatest good for the greatest number."	Costs and benefits can too easily be manipulated to justify our views. History shows that the majority rule principle means minority rights can be ignored.
Dialogic Ethics	Israel and France (1930s–1960s)	Martin Buber, *I and Thou* and Emmanuel Levinas, *Totality and Infinity: An Essay on Exteriority*	Locates ethical responsibility in the communicative relationships between people considered equal in value. There is a genuine desire to understand the other.	Requires listening and being vulnerable in communication, causing some to feel inadequate and/or uncertain about its usefulness. Setting aside one's ego or position in a relationship is demanding. Others may not respond in like fashion.

	Origins	Popularizing Figure and Famous Text	Evaluative Criteria	Criticisms
Feminist Ethics	France and USA (1940s–1980s)	Simone de Beauvoir, *The Second Sex* and Carol Gilligan, *In a Different Voice*	Considers personal connections as central through an ethic of care. Aims to understand, criticize, and correct how gender operates to advance equality and equity.	Centered on a gender binary when class, race, age, and ethnicity may also be important features of ethics. Impartiality and rationality are de-emphasized. May work against the ultimate goal of liberation when women are viewed as caregivers.
Media Ethics	1980s–1990s	Clifford Christians, *Responsibility in Mass Communications*	Media requires examination and judgment as an integral part of our social relationships, influencing our experiences of building and sustaining human community.	Respecting the rights of the public to know can sacrifice the rights of the individual to privacy. The media wields too much power in public discourse. Establishing what is the truth and who determines that, is challenging.

Chapter Activities

What's in a Name?

Your name is more than what people refer to you as; it actually tells a story about your values, cultural background, and a sense of who you are. This activity gives you a chance to explore this aspect of your identity, introduce yourself to your class, and importantly, learn about others' stories, values, and background in preparation for your journey in communication ethics during this class.

Misconduct at Alligator River

It is almost impossible to think about a college course on ethics without remembering an exercise much like *Alligator River* as a standout memory. This is an exercise that stresses the importance of seeking to understand different ethical perspectives by bringing them into conversation with each other. The activity encourages you to recognize ambiguity and complexity while focusing on reasoning and justification and letting go of the need for a correct answer.

The 42 Laws of Maat

Perhaps of all the foundational approaches, *Maat* is least studied and for this reason was especially chosen to appear in this volume. Taking on inclusiveness sometimes requires that we become willing to question some of our most basic assumptions, in order to make room for updated knowledge on the human quest to define the good. For while, the ancient Greeks have been the focus of discussions of classical approaches, African predecessors made contributions of their own that ought to be included. The goal is not to put ancient views on ethics in competition but instead to help you learn the many ways in which through commerce and politics these ancient civilizations learned from one another.

How Well do You Know Yourself?

A large part of philosophical thinking is learning about ourselves. After all, we are part of humanity, so understanding who we are helps us gain insight from others, at least in a small way. This activity guides you through a series of introspective questions that ask you consider your knowledge, values, skills, and behaviors in the context of both your past and your hopeful future.

References

Anderson, R., Baxter, L. Al, & Cissna, K. N. (2004). *Dialogue: Theorizing difference in communication studies.* Sage Publications.

Arnett, R. C. (1986). *Communication and community: Implications of Martin Buber's dialogue.* Southern Illinois University Press.

Arnett, R. C., Arneson, P., & Bell, L. M. (2006). Communication ethics: The dialogic turn. *Review of Communication, 6,* 63–93.

Arnett, R. C., Fritz, J. M. H., & Bell, L. M. (2009). *Communication ethics literacy: Dialogue and difference.* Sage Publications.

Ballard, R. L., Hoffer, M., & Bell McManus, L. M. (2016). Communication ethics: A vital resource in an ever-changing world. *Choice: Current Reviews for Academic Libraries, 54,* 155–164.

Benhabib, S. (1992). *Situating the self: Gender, community, and postmodernism in contemporary ethics.* Routledge.

Brislin, R. W., & Kim, E. S. (2003). Cultural diversity in people's understanding and uses of time. *Applied Psychology, 52*(3), 363–382. doi:10.1111/1464-0597.00140

Buber, M. (1970). *I and thou.* Simon & Schuster.

Christians, C. G., Fackler, M., McGee, K., Kreshel, P., & Woods, R. (2020). *Media ethics: Cases and moral reasoning* (11th ed.). Routledge.

Christians, C., & Traber, M. (1997). *Communication ethics and universal values.* Sage.

Dainton, M., & Zelley, E. D. (2019). *Applying communication theory for professional life: A practical introduction* (4th ed.). Sage.

Gilligan, C. (1982). *In a different voice: Psychological theory and women's development.* Harvard University Press (Reprint edition 2016).

Griffin, E., Ledbetter, A. M., & Sparks, G. G. (2018). *A first look at communication theory* (10th ed.). McGraw-Hill.

Held, V. (Ed.). (1995). *Justice and care: Essential readings in feminist ethics.* Westview Press.

hooks, b. (2014). *Ain't I a woman: Black women and feminism* (2nd ed.). Routledge.

Hyde, M. J. (2001). *The call of conscience: Heidegger and Levinas, rhetoric and the euthanasia debate.* University of South Carolina Press.

Jovanovic, S. (2008). Community as ethical expression: How discourse shapes a vision of hope. *Bridges: An Interdisciplinary Journal of Theology, Philosophy, History, and Sciences, 15*(1/2), 135–157.

Kohlberg, L. (1976). Moral stages and moralization: The cognitive developmental approach. In T. Lickona (Ed.). *Moral development and behavior* (pp. 31–53). Holt, Rinehart, & Winston.

Levinas, E. (1985). *Ethics and infinity* (R. A. Cohen, Trans.). Duquesne University Press.

MacIntyre, A. (2007). *After virtue* (3rd ed.). University of Notre Dame Press.

Manning, R. C. (1992). *Speaking from the heart.* Rowman & Littlefield.

Noddings, N. (2013). *Caring: A relational approach to ethics and moral education* (2nd ed.). University of California.

Nussbaum, M. (2013). Non-relative virtues: An Aristotelian approach. In R. Shafer-Landau (Ed.), *Ethical theory: An anthology* (2nd ed., pp. 630–644). Wiley-Blackwell.

Ortega y Gasset, J. (2000). *Meditations on Quixote*. University of Illinois Press (Originally published 1914)

Plaisance, P. (Ed.). (2018). *Communication and media ethics*. De Gruyter Mouton.

Rand, A. (1992). *Atlas shrugged.* Signet. (Original work published 1957)

Singer, P. (2015). *Animal liberation: The definitive class of the animal movement.* Open Road.

Ward, S. J. (2011). *Ethics and the media: An introduction.* Cambridge University Press.

Additional Resources

Communication Ethics Textbooks

Arnett, R., Fritz, J. M. H., & Bell McManus, L. M. (2018). *Communication ethics literacy: Dialogue and difference* (2nd ed.). Kendall Hunt.

Johannesen, R. L., Valde, K. S., & Whedbee, K. E. (2008). *Ethics in human communication* (6th ed). Waveland.

Neher, W. W., & Sandin, P. J. (2017). *Communicating ethically: Character, duties, consequences, and relationships* (2nd ed.). Routledge.

Tompkins, P. S. (2019). *Practicing communication ethics: Development, discernment, and decision making* (2nd ed.). Routledge.

Ethical Perspectives—Overviews

Anderson, R., Baxter, L. A., & Cissna, K. N. (2004). *Dialogue: Theorizing difference in communication studies.* Sage.

Arnett, R. C. (2017). *Levinas's rhetorical demand: The unending obligation of communication ethics.* Southern Illinois University Press.

Ballard, R. L. (2017). Communication ethics. In M. Allen (Ed.), *The Sage encyclopedia of communication research methods* (pp. 195–198). Sage Publications. Overview.

Berzin, A. (2011). Applying Buddhist principles for the age of social media: Unedited transcript. Berzin Archives. http://www.berzinarchives.com/web/en/archives/approaching_buddhism/world_today/appl_bst_principles_age_soc_media/transcript.html

Ishii, S. (2009). Conceptualising Asian communication ethics: A Buddhist perspective. *Journal of Multicultural Discourses, 4*(1), 49–60.

Lipari, L. (2009). Ethics theories. In S. Littlejohn & K. Foss (Eds.), *Encyclopedia of communication theory* (pp. 353–356). SAGE Publications. Overview.

Mowlana, H. (2007). Theoretical perspectives on Islam and communication. *China Media Research, 3*(4), 23–33.

Norlock, K. (2019). Feminist ethics. *Stanford Encyclopedia of Philosophy*. https://plato.stanford.edu/entries/feminism-ethics/Overview

Plaisance, P. (2009). Media ethics theories. In S. Littlejohn & K. Foss (Eds.), *Encyclopedia of communication theory* (pp. 638–642). SAGE Publications.

Wong, P. (2013). Confucian social media: An oxymoron? *Dao, 12,* 283–296.

Ethical Perspectives—Original Works

Aristotle. (350 B.C.E.). *Nicomachean ethics* (W. D. Ross, Trans.). https://socialsciences.mcmaster.ca/econ/ugcm/3ll3/aristotle/Ethics.pdf. This is a good free translation of the original work, but if you search for "Nicomachean Ethics pdf" or just "Nicomachean Ethics" online you will find many sources.

Kant, I. (1785). *Fundamental principles of the metaphysics of morals* (T. K. Abbott & P. McPherson Rudisill, Trans.). https://kantwesley.com/Kant/FndtnlPrncpMetaphsicMorals.pdf

Kant, I. (1785). *On a supposed right to lie because of philanthropic concerns* (T. K. Abbot, Trans.). https://pdfs.semanticscholar.org/aae1/988d5c2b465091316993bd1d1ecbddc26940.pdf

Mill, J. S. (1863). *Utilitarianism.* Kitchener, ON: Batoche Books (2001). http://socserv.mcmaster.ca/econ/ugcm/3ll3/mill/utilitarianism.pdf. This is a good free translation of the original work, but if you search for "Utilitarianism Ethics pdf" or just "Utilitarianism" online you will find many sources.

Videos

Christians, C. G. (2013). Truth in the age of global media. [Video]. YouTube. Presented at American University in Bulgaria. https://youtu.be/xO7ZeImoCgU [about an hour and a half]

Dodson, E. L. (2014). Buber in 10 minutes. [Video]. YouTube. https://youtu.be/16Cr82mLhkw [about 10 minutes]

Ethics Unwrapped. (2017). Deontology. [Video]. McCombs School of Business. The University of Texas at Austin. https://ethicsunwrapped.utexas.edu/glossary/deontology [Between 1 and 2 minutes]

Ethics Unwrapped. (2017). Moral Imagination. [Video]. McCombs School of Business. The University of Texas at Austin. https://ethicsunwrapped.utexas.edu/glossary/moral-imagination [Between 1 and 2 minutes]

Ethics Unwrapped. (2017). Moral Psychology. [Video]. McCombs School of Business. The University of Texas at Austin. https://ethicsunwrapped.utexas.edu/glossary/moral-psychology [Between 1 and 2 minutes]

Ethics Unwrapped. (2017). Utilitarianism. [Video]. McCombs School of Business. The University of Texas at Austin. https://ethicsunwrapped.utexas.edu/glossary/utilitarianism [Between 1 and 2 minutes]

Ethics Unwrapped. (2017). Values. [Video]. McCombs School of Business. The University of Texas at Austin. https://ethicsunwrapped.utexas.edu/glossary/values [Between 1 and 2 minutes]

Ethics Unwrapped. (2017). Virtue ethics. [Video]. McCombs School of Business. The University of Texas at Austin. https://ethicsunwrapped.utexas.edu/glossary/virtue-ethics [Between 1 and 2 minutes]

Gilligan, C. (2012). Carol Gilligan on women and moral development. Big Think. https://youtu.be/2W_9MozRoKE [about 6 minutes]

What's in a Name?

How Our Names Offer a Window into Ethical and Cultural Values

Most of us are named by our parents or caregivers at birth. Sometimes, an older brother or sister gets the honor of offering a name. Some of those who name us participate in cultural practices that may reflect deep values that go back many generations. Others who name us may opt for tapping into current popular culture ideas. Thus, inquiring into a person's name can supply us with important information about the beliefs, attitudes, and ethics of another person's family values, attitudes, and customs.

In the Chinese culture, names are chosen based on a particular set of character traits that are highly valued and which the parents wish to manifest in their children. These names usually mean something that is admired in a given cultural context. This is a way to proclaim the child's individuality while connecting symbolically with existing cultural meanings. On the other hand, in some Western cultures, including the United States and England, babies are sometimes named after celebrities, brand names, and literary characters (Lorenz, 1989). This is indicative of a value of hierarchy that privileges success and fame. For example, a 2016 British consumer analytics study found that, "It is not uncommon for influential celebrities' baby names to gain popularity: for example, over 96% of persons named Brooklyn in the United Kingdom are younger than [professional model] Brooklyn Beckham" (Lansley & Longley, 2016, p. 274).

Alternatively, other cultures place an emphasis on the continuity of families. For example, a baby named after her grandmother Melba was a way to honor and extend the elder's legacy. Sociologist Janet Finch (2008) reflects on this practice this way: "If firstborn children are seen as the ones who create a new generation, then there is a special significance in naming them in a way which makes connections with previous generations" (p. 720). Finch is emphatic on this point: "Changes in the popularity of different names over time have been capitalized in the development of a social research tool which can predict the statistical probability that someone with a specific name falls into a particular age group" (p. 719).

In short, whether personal naming is a tool to assert kinship or point to a preferred popular name, the very act of our being named is quite telling of the kind of cultural values, social networks, and customs that influence our moral development. By observing the origins of names of those around us, we gain insight into ours and others' formative environments while acknowledging that as people mature, they may embrace those formative values, be indifferent to them, or even reject them for a number of reasons. For instance:

> When Cassius Clay changed his name to Muhammad Ali soon after he had won the world heavyweight boxing championship, he did so in order to distance himself from the history of slavery which his birth name denoted, and to embrace the identity of the Muslim faith in a particular form, the Nation of Islam. All adherents to the Nation of Islam ceased using their former surnames, sometimes declining to adopt any alternative, as was the case with the then leader of the movement, Malcolm X (Finch, 2008, p. 713).

Do you know how you got your name? If not, is there a family member you can ask to hear the story? Or, can you do research on your own to learn of your name's connection to culture, relatives, and values?

In this activity, you will increase your *knowledge* by considering:

- How well do you know the origin of your name?

- Does it reflect a connection with a particular culture, kinship, pop culture, religion, or ancestral history?

In this activity, you will learn *skills* by asking yourself:

- Are you able to pick up on the cultural factors that influence the selection of a name?

- Are you able to make inferences about the values and cultural background of people based on their names while allowing for the possibility that they may adhere, may be indifferent to, or may have rebelled against those values?

In this activity, you will reflect on your own *values* by asking:

- What benefits can you articulate to inquiring into others' names?

- How might you ask about names and values of acquaintances, friends, co-workers, romantic interests?

- How might being attuned to others' names cultivate closer relationships and understanding of others, their culture, and their values?

In this activity, you can take *action* by assessing:

- How good is your ability to collect qualitative data on ethics and culture through listening to others tell the stories of their given names?

- What biases or difficulties can you uncover in your own thinking as you become attuned to your peers and their stories of names?

The Activity

Tell the class about the origin of your name.

Discussion Questions

1. How do you feel about the name that was assigned to you?

2. As you listened to your peers, did you notice any patterns regarding the origins of their names? Were names chosen primarily for religious, connectedness, or individual identity factors?

3. Did anything surprise you about the stories shared by your peers?

4. What particular stories were you more easily able to relate? Which ones least? Why?

5. How does your own naming origin, as well as value formation, compare to others?

References

Finch, J. (2008). Naming names: Kinship, individuality and personal names. *Sociology, 42*(4), 709–725.

Lansley, G., & Longley, P. (2016). Deriving age and gender from forenames for consumer analytics. *Journal of Retailing and Consumer Services, 30*, 271–278.

Lorenz, B. (1989). Origins of unusual given names from the Southern United States. *Names: A Journal of Onomastics, 37*(3), 201–230.

Misconduct at Alligator River

Justifying Values and Using Ethical Perspectives

So many perspectives! How do we make sense of them all? When learning ethics, you probably feel overwhelmed by all the different ethical perspectives. One perspective focuses on principles, another on outcomes, another on how we treat one another, and more. So which one is right? Which one do you use?

We can't tell you which one to use—that's the part of ethical thinking that requires wisdom and experience. But what we can show you is how to apply them, and more importantly, how to apply multiple perspectives to a single situation, use them to help justify decisions, and show you how they reveal different perspectives and different points of view.

In this activity, you will increase your *knowledge* by considering:

- How much of, and how many of the ethical perspectives do you recall?

In this activity, you will learn *skills* by asking yourself:

- How can you apply a variety of ethical perspectives to one situation?
- How can you engage in perspective taking using the ethical perspectives you have learned?
- How can you make an ethical choice and justify it?
- How can you learn to become more comfortable with making trade-offs and ambiguity, as ethical thinking requires?

In this activity, you will reflect on your *values* by questioning:

- Which ethical perspective do you align with the most and why?
- How does that ethical perspective help you justify your values and ethical sensibility?
- What perspectives do not seem to resonate with you and why?

In this activity, you will be able to take action by asking:

- How can you apply a variety of ethical perspectives to your own ethical dilemmas?
- How can ethical perspectives help you understand why others make the choices they do, even if you disagree?

The Activity

This activity provides an excellent introduction to applying the ethical perspectives presented earlier in this chapter.

Part I:

Read the short story, "Alligator River" (it's only one page long).

Part II:

Respond in short answer form to the discussion questions about the story characters and their actions.

Alligator River[1]

In the sylvan setting of the land of Ethos runs the sinuous Alligator River, named for the reptiles who populate its water and banks and who dine upon any local denizens unfortunate enough to fall into their gaping maws. On one side of the river lives Sylvia: sensitive, demure, and chaste. Across the river lives Hector, Sylvia's love, proud and strong in spirit and mind. No wall of stone or statute more effectively separated this Thisbe from her Pyramus than did the Alligator River. No Hero pined more for her Leander, no Juliet longed more for her Romeo, than did Sylvia for her Hector.

Independent and resourceful, Sylvia was determined to discover a means of transporting herself safely across the Alligator River to join her lover Hector. Sylvia's first encounter in her quest was with Sinbad, the Sailor. Sylvia explained to Sinbad her plight, testified to him aloud her great love for Hector, and implored Sinbad to lend her his boat, the only means of transport across the river. Sinbad, opportunistic and wanton, agreed to the loan of his boat upon the condition that Sylvia first spend the night with him.

Sylvia's indignation at Sinbad's promiscuous proposition and its challenging of her chastity and of the fidelity to Hector provoked her to tears, and she turned from Sinbad in anger to pursue other alternatives for crossing the river.

Still distraught, Sylvia next encountered Ivan, the Uninvolved, to whom she related her predicament and Sinbad the Sailor's coarse recommendation to her. Ivan listened impatiently, and a slight frown of disdain crossed his face as he issued forth his reaction: "Don't bother me with your problems, Sylvia; I've enough to worry about myself without carrying the burden of your petty hardships."

Separation from Hector was hardly a petty consideration for Sylvia, however, and she departed Ivan more hurt and distressed than ever. Confused, lovesick, and dispirited, Sylvia decided reluctantly to return to Sinbad to accept his bargain, rationalizing that the end, being with her lover Hector, justified the means, compromising her fidelity and chastity. Sinbad the Sailor, true to his bargain, accepted Sylvia into his cabin for the night and lent her his boat the following day so that Sylvia soon crossed the Alligator River for a joyful reunion with Hector. Hector welcomed Sylvia into his arms, for he loved and admired her deeply. For one full day Hector and Sylvia enjoyed the blissful peace of their warm and tender regard for one another. Yet soon Sylvia, nagged by her conscience for the expedient she had adopted for realizing her purpose, admitted to Hector the tough bargain Sinbad had insisted upon.

Hector was not sympathetic. In fact, his rage at Sylvia's betrayal of him culminated in his casting aside of Sylvia, vowing never again to look at her for her infidelity. Sylvia's remorse, shame, and dejection at Hector's reaction soon festered into rage at his harsh lack of understanding. As Sylvia wandered about, she happened upon Atlas, who listened to her story and completely empathized with Sylvia's ire at Hector: in fact, Atlas suggested that Sylvia retaliate against Hector. She agreed, and Atlas assumed upon his shoulders the task of becoming the agent of Hector's punishment. Sylvia led Atlas back to Hector, and Atlas brutally beat Hector, a spectacle that was accompanied by Sylvia's scornful laughter, for now she had bruised Hector physically as he had bruised her emotionally.

---

[1] Adapted from https://www.nais.org/articles/pages/moral-education-on-the-banks-of-the-alligator-rive/

Discussion Questions:

1. **Virtue ethics** asks: "What kind of person do I want to be?" What kind of person does Atlas want to be? What virtues would you identify in Atlas? Would you agree or disagree with his virtues? In what ways did Atlas go too far in exhibiting his virtues, or not enough?

2. **Duty ethics** encourages us to consider two questions: "What is the right thing to do?" where right is the same for all people, in all situations; and "How can we treat others as ends in themselves, rather than means to some other end?" How did Hector fail to meet these expectations of duty ethics? What other characters treated others as means and not ends and thereby violated duty ethics?

3. **Consequentialist ethics** encourages us to ask: "What is the greatest good for the greatest number?" In what ways did Sinbad abide by, or fail to abide by consequentialist ethics? Additionally, how did Sylvia justify spending the night with Sinbad using consequentialist ethics?

4. **Dialogic ethics** asks us: "How do I value and include the other?" When Sylvia admitted her choice to Hector, he was not sympathetic and went into a rage. If Hector had employed a dialogic ethics approach, how might have he responded instead?

5. **Feminist ethics** encourages us to consider: "How can I demonstrate care and minimize harm for self and others?" Did Ivan's position of non-involvement minimize harms? How could Ivan have followed a feminist ethics approach in responding to Sylvia? Additionally, does Sylvia demonstrate care for Hector and minimize harm by rejecting Sinbad?

6. If you read this story in the newspaper, would that change your understanding? Would you immediately think of ethical questions? What kinds of questions might you ask instead? What if you saw this story on Facebook with a before picture of Sylvia and Hector madly in love and an after picture of Atlas beating up Hector and Sylvia laughing at him? How might you interpret it differently then? Considering these – a news story or Facebook post – how does media influence human community, understanding, and response?

7. One aspect of philosophical thinking as it relates to communication ethics is appreciating and distinguishing between multiple ways of defining the good. After answering some of the above questions, how are you developing this skill and considering the good in multiple ways?

8. Culture, ontology, inclusion, and consistency are also part of ethical thinking.

   a. Culture – If this was a culture where open relationships (i.e., not monogamous ones – one person with one person) were valued, how might you interpret the ethical dilemmas and perspectives in Alligator River differently?

   b. Ontology – In looking at the characters in Alligator River, what stands out as a common good as the basis of ethical reasoning? For instance, do the characters value caring for others or self, most of all? Is honesty highly regarded? How is gender equality valued, or not?

   c. Inclusion – How did each character exhibit or fail to be inclusive?

   d. Consistency – Which character do you think acted most consistently from an ethical standpoint? From which ethical perspective did that character act?

Complete the Following Steps:

1. Identify which ethical perspective(s) each character in the story used in making decisions and choices. The characters are Sylvia, Hector, Sinbad, Ivan, and Atlas.

2. Rank each character from most ethical to the least ethical (1 most ethical to 5 least ethical). Then, note which ethical perspective you used to justify and support your ranking. There may not be any ties.

3. Your instructor will provide you with the next set of instructions for how to use your rankings.

The 42 Laws of Maat

Contemporary Ideas About Rightness and Wrongness Have a Millenia-Old History

One of the most fascinating aspects of studying ancient approaches to ethics is the realization that ancient cultures were linked through commerce and conquest, and thus influenced each other's beliefs, values, and ethics. The 42 Laws of Maat (see below) of ancient Egypt are a testament to our human propensity to shape each other's ideas. To be good students of communication ethics, we must take an interest in the historical and cultural origins of our commonly held beliefs about the nature of rightness and wrongness. By going back in time, we can learn how human ideas about morality have morphed and changed through the years, depending on cultural contexts and historical situations. Importantly, by going back centuries or even millennia, we find that human communication has been at the center of what it means to be a good or virtuous person since humans began recording their lives. Thus, engaging foundational approaches to ethics facilitates our ability to make meaningful connections between ethics and the particular material and historical circumstances that make certain values popular at different times in history.

While much of the literature on ethics traces its study to ancient Greece, more recent scholarship in Egyptology, Africana Studies, anthropology, and communication ethics has traced that history to

Symbols of Ancient Egyptian

© Liudmila Klymenko/Shutterstock.com

millennia before Jesus Christ in the form of ancient African approaches to ethics. In spite of the discovery of the Instructions of Ptahhotep by French archeologists in Thebes in 1858, it took another century for its content to be recognized as the oldest treatise on ethics discovered to date (Simpson, 1986).

As the location of some of the first civilizations on earth, African people began to organize themselves socially in a way that allowed large numbers of people to dwell, co-exist, and share resources in a sustainable fashion. This shift to communal city life was propelled by developments in agriculture that permitted previously nomadic herding groups to settle in larger aggregates with more secure sources of food and shelter. In short, as humanity transitioned from pastoral lifestyles into cosmopolitan ones, certain values such as collaboration, listening, and mutual respect rose to the list of priorities in order to ensure peaceful and productive co-existence in newly densely populated urban city centers like Punt and Nubia, which maintained both political and commercial relationships with Egypt.

In this activity, you will increase your *knowledge* by considering:

- What contributions have ancient African people made to human ethics?

- What ancient or contemporary ideas about virtue and vice are evident in the 42 Laws of Maat?

- How do you see the influence of the 42 Laws of Maat today?

- How do the 42 Laws of Maat reflect different ethical perspectives?

In this activity, you will learn *skills* by asking yourself:

- What practical skills do you see evolving from the 42 Laws of Maat?

- How do virtues such as honesty and obedience manifest themselves to facilitate peaceful coexistence?

- How does the practice of Maat compare to other Western views on ethics such as duty, feminist, consequentialist, or virtue ethics?

In this activity, you will reflect on your own *values* by exploring:

- What ethical values do the 42 Laws of Maat promote?

- Which of the values in the 42 Laws of Matt do you believe are still relevant or no longer relevant to life in the 21st century?

In this activity, you could take *action* by critically questioning:

- Do you see a connection between the values promoted in the 42 Laws of Maat and Egypt's cultural longevity?

- In what ways do you think the 42 Laws of Maat contributed to sustaining Egypt's 3,000-year reign?

The Activity

Part 1: In small groups, you will be assigned some of the 42 Laws of Maat for your group to read and discuss its connection to contemporary laws, religious beliefs, cultural values, and ethical approaches. You will be asked if these laws resemble in any way the values that we hold today.

Part 2: Share with the class what surprised you most about this activity and what connections to the present your group found most interesting.

Maatian Ethics

Also known as the 42 Negative Confessions, ancient Egyptian ideas about morality predate Aristotle by at least 2,000 years and the Ten Commandments by 1,000 years. Ptahhotep was a vizier (high official) who is believed to have been 110 years old when he wrote *The Maxims of Ptahhotep* in 2375 BCE as a guide to his descendants on how to live a righteous life. Egyptians did not have a concept of religion, but they had a fully developed concept of moral accountability that they called Maat. This may come as a surprise to some readers as the Hollywood version of ancient Egyptians depicts them as engaged in cult-like religious obsession, but Maat was also the Egyptian divinity which they represented as a woman with bird wings widespread and holding a scale. While ideas about heaven or hell were not known to ancient Egyptians, they believed that life continued after death and those who behaved morally possessed a heart that was lighter than a feather at the time of death. It was Maat's job to weigh each person's heart after death to determine if they would go on to exist in a different form forever (Neter) or would be forgotten.

In chapter 125 of *The Papyrus of Ani,* archeologists uncovered a complete list of the 42 Negative Confessions (moral laws). It was called a negative confession because every Egyptian citizen was encouraged to voice to themselves in the affirmative in the mornings ("I will not") and repeat as a negative confession ("I have not") every evening. Below is Budge's public domain translation of the 42 Divine laws of Maat in their negative articulation (Ptahhotep, 1986):

1. I have not committed wrongs.

2. I have not committed robbery with violence.

3. I have not stolen.

4. I have not slain men or women.

5. I have not stolen food.

6. I have not swindled offerings.

7. I have not stolen from divine spirits.

8. I have not told lies.

9. I have not carried away food.

10. I have not cursed.

11. I have not closed my ears to truth.

12. I have not committed adultery.

13. I have not made anyone cry.

14. I have not felt sorrow without reason.

15. I have not assaulted anyone.

16. I am not deceitful.

17. I have not stolen anyone's land.

18. I have not been an eavesdropper.

19. I have not falsely accused anyone.

20. I have not been angry without reason.

21. I have not seduced anyone's wife.

22. I have not polluted myself.

23. I have not terrorized anyone.

24. I have not disobeyed the law.

25. I have not been exclusively angry.

26. I have not cursed divine spirits.

27. I have not behaved with violence.

28. I have not caused disruption of peace.

29. I have not acted hastily or without thought.

30. I have not overstepped my boundaries of concern.

31. I have not exaggerated my words when speaking.

32. I have not worked evil.

33. I have not used evil thoughts, words, or deeds.

34. I have not polluted the water.

35. I have not spoken angrily or arrogantly.

36. I have not cursed anyone in thought, word, or deeds.

37. I have not placed myself on a pedestal.

38. I have not stolen what belongs to divine spirits.

39. I have not stolen from or disrespected the deceased.

40. I have not taken food from a child.

41. I have not acted with insolence.

42. I have not destroyed property belonging to divine spirits.

References

Budge, E. A. W. (1967). *The book of the dead: The papyrus of ani in the British museum*. Dover Publications, Inc.

Simpson, W. K., (Ed.). (1986). The maxims of Ptahhotep. In *The literature of ancient Egypt: An anthology of stories, instructions, stelae, autobiographies, and poetry*. Yale University Press.

Additional Resources

Karenga, M. (2004). *Maat, the moral ideal of ancient Egypt: A study in classical African ethics*. Routledge.

Vélez Ortiz, M. (2020). *Maatian ethics in a communication context*. Routledge.

How Well Do You Know Yourself?

A Question for All Human Beings

The inscription *know thyself* was a common feature of ancient Egyptian temples, including the magnificent temple in Luxor built by the legendary architect, physician, and philosopher Amenhotep III (1390–1352 BC) who reigned Egypt from 1390 to 53 BCE. A thousand years later (~7 BC), the same inscription was also featured prominently in the Temple of Apollo at Delphi, Athens. The presence and social significance of this ethical imperative in classical civilizations places our individual quest for self-knowledge at the very center of what it means to be ethical, in communication and otherwise.

Three centuries later in the 4th century BC, Aristotle (384 BC to 322 BC) made the connection between individual self-knowledge and ethicality explicit in his writings about virtue ethics. By design, virtue ethics encourages you to look into your community and within yourself as you select a model citizen on which to base your own character. Through this process, you, as a moral agent, engage in a constant negotiation of particular needs and values. Such negotiation succeeds when you reflect on your own virtues and vices in order to make improvements and modifications where needed.

While some have criticized the flexibility a virtues approach to ethics offers, others are drawn to it precisely because it eschews a focus on laws and consequences in favor of a personal, reflective quest for truth and meaning. It recognizes the diversity of individuals even within the same culture while also pointing to the art of ethics, over science. And, it points toward the need for ongoing, personal reflection.

© StunningArt/Shutterstock.com

In order for your daily actions to help you achieve your goals, you must first examine your commitments and how you articulate them to other people. This activity will help you search within for your ideal self. It will also help you practice how to articulate that vision of yourself to others.

In this activity, you will increase your *knowledge* by considering:

- How do you see yourself in relation to the community and the rest of humankind?
- What are virtues according to Aristotle?
- What do you consider to be your virtues?
- What is your current ideal version of yourself?
- How do you see yourself in relation to the community and the rest of humankind?

In this activity, you will reflect on your own *values* by asking:

- How would you describe your values and commitments?
- Are there social issues or causes to which you see yourself as an advocate?
- How would you like others to remember you when you are gone?
- What kind of society would be created based on your personal values and commitments?
- Are there any problems with your values and commitments from a societal standpoint?

In this activity, you will learn *skills* by asking yourself:

- What ethical skills or practices have you adopted or considered adopting from someone you hold in high esteem?
- Why are those skills and practices ones you consider important?
- Have you consciously attempted to become like one of your role models? If so, who?
- Why and how did you choose your particular role model(s)?
- How can you realistically assess your strengths and weaknesses?

In this activity, you can take *action* by assessing:

- What are you actively doing to improve your character and communication?
- How do you manifest your values in your community and the world?
- Do your actions match your values?

The Activity

After watching the short (7:20) video titled *Cornel West on Courage*, featuring contemporary ethicist Dr. Cornel West (2008), write meaningful answers to the following three questions (https://www.youtube.com/watch?v=YYRuqDnyoBg).

- What kind of human being do you want to be?
- What kind of legacy do you want to leave behind?
- What kind of witness do you want to bear? (e.g., For whom will you advocate?)

References

Aminyamout. (2011, May 24). *Cornel West on courage*. [Video]. YouTube. https://www.youtube.com/watch?v=YYRuqDnyoBg

West, C. (2008). *Hope on a tightrope: Words & wisdom*. Smiley Books.

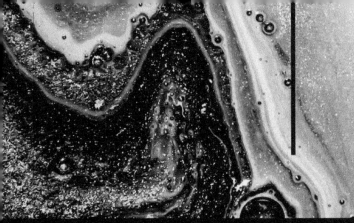

Interpersonal Communication Ethics

When Kim met her roommate at the new student orientation, they connected immediately and found they shared the same major and interests. However, now in their third month as roommates, there is some tension. As the person known as the life of the party, Sandy invites friends over until late into the night, drinks heavily, and smokes in the room. At first, Kim liked her roommate's outgoing personality because she met new people, but she quickly realized the partying lifestyle conflicted with her values to do well academically. How should Kim respond to Sandy? Is it okay for her not to say anything to Sandy even though the parties are straining their relationship? If Kim asks the resident assistant for help, would she violate Sandy's trust? These are some of the questions we ask in interpersonal communication ethics. In this chapter, we consider the intersection of interpersonal communication and communication ethics. We will briefly summarize the history, theoretical perspectives, and topics of interpersonal communication research. Next, we describe how communication ethics informs the development of interpersonal communication ethics and introduce the activities in this chapter.

Generally, scholars agree interpersonal communication focuses on communication between two people who experience face-to-face communication in an ongoing relationship (Neher & Sandin, 2007). Neher and Sandin (2007) define interpersonal as live, face-to-face communication that is not mediated, for example, by texting or social media posts. We acknowledge that much of our communication happens over a phone or computer, but an interpersonal relationship requires some face-to-face communication.

In the 1960s, the study of interpersonal communication gained traction when psychiatry shifted its focus from intrapersonal to interpersonal and when the Civil Rights Movement for Black Americans and the United States' involvement in the Vietnam War ultimately led younger generations to

© fizkes/Shutterstock.com

see their personal fulfillment connected to their relationships (Knapp & Daly, 2011). Over the next decade, interpersonal communication began to flourish with an increase in university faculty integrating interpersonal concepts in their courses, the publication of textbooks, and professional organizations creating interest groups focused on interpersonal communication (Knapp & Daly, 2011). Interpersonal communication gained credibility as an area of academic study and grew in strength and reputation on college campuses.

Trends in Interpersonal Communication Scholarship

Over the last 50 years, interpersonal communication scholars' theoretical perspectives have expanded and range from dialogic, social exchange, uncertainty reduction, social, communibiological, and intercultural communication (Arnett et al., 2018, p. 115). Moreover, some of the topics being studied by interpersonal communication researchers include personality, knowledge, biology and physiology, language, nonverbal behavior, emotion, supportive communication, social networks, interpersonal influence, interpersonal conflict, computer-mediated communication, interpersonal skills, interpersonal communication in the workplace, intercultural perspectives, romantic relationships, health care, family communication, and lifespan communication (Knapp & Daly, 2011).

As scholars pursued interpersonal communication research, Keller and Brown (1968) applied psychological theory to the relationship between the speaker and listener and introduced an interpersonal communication ethic. They suggest when a speaker respects a listener's freedom to choose how to respond to a message, it is more ethical; by contrast, when the speaker's reaction to the listener constrains his/her independence, it is considered less ethical (p. 79). The authors further the development of interpersonal communication through their consideration of the attitudes and feelings of the speaker and listener.

Although Keller and Brown contribute to an initial understanding of ethics in interpersonal communication, Fritz (2016) identifies the need for additional scholarship to address interpersonal communication ethics. She delineates how some interpersonal scholars researched ethics in interpersonal communication from a social scientific perspective (Knapp & Daly, 2011; Littlejohn & Jabusch, 1982; Planalp & Fitness, 2011) and how communication ethics scholars, working from a dialogic perspective, provide additional understanding of interpersonal communication ethics.

Interpersonal Communication Ethics

As we consider the intersection of interpersonal communication and communication ethics, our goal is not to tell you what to think but to prompt how to think about ethical questions in relationships with others. Scholars of interpersonal communication ethics ask: Is it ever okay to lie to friends, family, or significant others? How do we listen ethically? What is the significance of acknowledgment for human well-being? Who do I want to be in this relationship? Returning to our opening scenario, if Sandy asks her roommate, "how are things going in our dorm room?" is it ethical for Kim to say she is fine or should she share her concerns about their living arrangement and how it is impacting her academically and personally?

To review, we define communication ethics "as a process of reasoning aimed at providing sound justifications for or against particular communication behaviors, choices, messages, and acts"

(Ballard et al., 2016, p. 155). In addition, the purpose of communication ethics is to apply a philosophy of communication to an understanding of the good in a given situation and see how it interacts with other ideas (Arnett et al., 2018, p. 30). Research topics vary widely among communication ethics scholars, which is discussed in detail in Chapter 1 of this book. Interpersonal communication ethics situates ethics in communication and relationships, and addresses ethical questions that arise when two people form a relationship.

Chapter Activities

We each have deeply held beliefs, values, and customs. Communication ethics empowers and equips us to learn from others who differ from us. The activities in this chapter introduce some of the perspectives foundational to communication ethics and include: *What is Dialogic Ethics: A Film Analysis Activity; Listening Otherwise; Life-Giving Gift of Acknowledgment: To See the Invisible Man; The Virtues of Identity; Reciprocity, Fairness, and Cooperation*; and *The Ethical Inevitability of Conflict*.

What is Dialogic Ethics? A Film Analysis Activity

In the first activity, we consider interpersonal communication ethics through the lens of dialogue. Here you have the opportunity to learn about philosopher Martin Buber's contribution to dialogic ethics. Buber (1970) distinguishes between communication from a self-focused perspective (I-It) and an other-oriented perspective (I-Thou). Through a film analysis, this activity shows how dialogic ethics prioritizes respecting and listening to others, being open to those who differ from us, communicating for understanding, and learning together. For instance, if we apply a dialogic perspective to the situation with Kim and Sandy, it could begin with them meeting at a campus café where they can listen to how each person is experiencing the shared room. For Kim, it means setting aside her bias that she has the right to a quiet room, putting aside blame, and striving to see Sandy as a unique human being. For Sandy, a dialogic perspective means being willing to suspend her assumption that Kim does not know how to enjoy college life. Dialogic ethics requires both roommates to be open to the moment and open to any communication it brings without an expectation of certain outcomes. Buber would urge Kim and Sandy to see the other as the unique person she is and seek to understand the other. Dialogic ethics calls us to be open to learning from those who differ from us. As a result, we will be better equipped to care for others in our lives.

Listening Otherwise

In this series, there are three activities on ethical listening. Rather than listening to evaluate (such as when you are watching a movie) or listening to appreciate (when attending a concert), ethical listening moves us to be aware of our own emotions and the emotions of others so we can identify with them. It also provides the opportunity to practice how to reduce distractions with technology and to be present to others. For instance, if Kim applies ethical listening, she would learn that Sandy has recently been placed on academic probation and is fearful she will not live up to her family's expectations. Kim would also learn Sandy's significant other broke up with her and she is trying to distract herself with partying to avoid grieving this loss. Although this is a hypothetical situation, we will encounter challenges with friends where this activity will be an important reminder to set our phones down so we can listen and empathize.

The Life-Giving Gift of Acknowledgment: To See the Invisible Man

The next activity introduces Michael Hyde's idea of the life-giving gift of acknowledgment. From a communication ethics perspective, this activity asks: "What is the important role communication plays in helping us feel alive, included, and acknowledged?" This activity shows why it is ethical to acknowledge another person by analyzing a television episode of *Twilight Zone* (Twilight Zone, 1986) entitled *To See an Invisible Man*. It asks us to think about how acknowledgment is a communicative act. Why is it life-giving? Holba (2008) adds to an understanding of the significance of acknowledgment. "Without acknowledgement we may fall as prey into the realm of a social death, where invisibility and hopelessness pervade all of human emotion" (p. 501). In our scenario, if Sandy and Kim are able to acknowledge each other, it could be a positive step for Kim to feel visible in her dorm room and for both to begin rebuilding their relationship.

The Virtues of Identity

The Virtues of Identity activity invites you to reflect on your values, virtues, roles, and social positions to understand your identities. What does society claim is virtuous about your social role or identity? This activity demonstrates the connection between identity formation, ethics, and communication. Drawing on the influential work of Aristotle and the Golden Mean, you have the opportunity to reflect on how you define your identity by considering your personality traits, cultural background, faith, and/or gender. If Kim and Sandy did this activity, for example, they would both identify as students. For Kim, this role symbolizes her goal to go to college and become a physical therapist. For Sandy, identifying the role of student brings a mix of feelings. Since her brothers earned scholarships to top universities, Sandy initially felt discouraged and now being placed on academic probation she is rethinking her identities. Through this activity, both Kim and Sandy would see how roles have some good and some bad, which are evaluations learned from our culture, media, and community. This activity provides awareness of how we socially construct our identities.

Reciprocity, Fairness, and Cooperation

This activity on reciprocity asks you to investigate fairness, cooperation, and the Golden Rule. What is fair? What is unfair? Is it fair to get something for free when others do not? What values or set of rules are associated with fairness? For instance, when Sandy and Kim pay the same amount for their room, is it fair for Sandy to use it for parties and for Kim to have to find a quiet place to study? Next, this activity invites you to consider the role of cooperation and ask what is the benefit of cooperation in relationships? How could Sandy and Kim cooperate in sharing their space? Finally, this activity asks how is reciprocity hardwired into us? What does the Golden Rule to treat others as we wish others to treat us mean in the 21st century? Practically, how could it benefit your relationships? The activities on reciprocity will enrich your knowledge of fairness, cooperation, and the Golden Rule.

The Ethical Inevitability of Conflict

In the activity, The Inevitability of Conflict, we invite you to think about previous conflict situations you have experienced. How was conflict communicated? How have your past experiences with conflict influenced how you communicate conflict today? Do you tend to avoid conflict like Kim or accommodate, compete, compromise, or collaborate when you encounter a conflict situation? This activity will provide an opportunity to reflect on your values and to increase your awareness of issues that create conflict situations. Finally, this activity will help you to recognize that everyone responds to conflict differently and to consider the ethical assumptions associated with specific conflicts.

We hope you will engage the activities in this chapter to think deeply about interpersonal communication ethics and to grow in your knowledge of self and others.

References

Arnett, R. C., Fritz, J. M. H., & Bell McManus, L. M. (2018). *Communication ethics literacy: Dialogue and difference* (2nd ed.). Kendall Hunt.

Ballard, R. L., Hoffer, M., & Bell McManus, L. M. (2016). Communication ethics: A vital resource in an ever-changing world. *Choice: Current Reviews for Academic Libraries, 54*, 155–164.

Buber, M. (1970). *I and thou*. Simon & Schuster.

Fritz, J. M. H. (2016). Interpersonal communication ethics. In C. R. Berger & M. E. Roloff (Eds.), *The international encyclopedia of interpersonal communication*. John Wiley & Sons, Inc. https://doi.org/10.1002/9781118540190.wbeic.227

Holba, A. (2008). Revisiting Martin Buber's I-It: A rhetorical strategy. *Human Communication, 11*(4), 495–510.

Keller, P. W., & Brown, C. T. (1968). An interpersonal ethic for communication. *The Journal of Communication, 18*, 78–81.

Knapp, M. L., & Daly, J. A. (2011). *The Sage handbook of interpersonal communication* (4th ed.). Sage.

Littlejohn, S. W., & Jabusch, D. M. (1982). Communication competence: Model and application. *Journal of Applied Communication Research, 10*(1), 19–37. https://doi.org/10.1080/00909888209365210

Neher, W. W., & Sandin, P. J. (2007). *Communicating ethically: Character, duties, consequences, and relationships*. Pearson Education, Inc.

Planalp, S., & Fitness, J. (2011). Interpersonal communication ethics. In G. Cheney, S. May, & D. Munshi (Eds.), *Handbook of communication ethics*. Taylor and Francis.

Twilight Zone. (1986, January 31, original air date). To see the invisible man. [Video] YouTube. https://www.youtube.com/watch?v=p0oPwt9n-38

What is Dialogic Ethics?

A Film Analysis Activity

In the 1960s, Black American women made significant contributions to Astronaut John Glenn's successful orbit of the earth through their work at the National Aeronautics and Space Administration (NASA). However, as the film *Hidden Figures* portrays, the state of Virginia was segregated at the time and racism was rampant. In the film, some white characters avoid eye contact with black characters, treat them like machines, and refuse to acknowledge their humanness. These are examples of I-It relationships. Through an analysis of *Hidden Figures*, this activity reviews philosopher Martin Buber's (1970) idea of I-It and I-Thou relationships. This activity also differentiates genuine dialogue, technical dialogue, and monologue in a discussion on dialogic ethics.

According to Buber, dialogue distinguishes communication from a self-focused perspective (I-It) to an other-oriented perspective (I-Thou). In Chapter 1, we explained Buber's suggestion that people relate to others on a continuum of I-It to I-Thou relationships. In an I-It relationship, the self sees the other as an object or instrument and is unable to recognize the uniqueness of the other.

By contrast, the ethical relation of I-Thou affirms the other person as a unique human being and allows genuine dialogue to occur. Genuine dialogue is evident when two people have mutual respect, commit to listen, and seek to learn from each other, particularly when they disagree. Here we imagine team members with divergent views being open to look at a situation from the other's perspective. When we have the ethical relationship of I-Thou, commit to learning, and remain open to the other, genuine dialogue can emerge.

Buber distinguishes a second type of communication, technical dialogue, which is evident in functional communication. For example, technical dialogue occurs when a professor encourages discussion to facilitate students' understanding of an idea. The third type of communication, monologue or monologic communication, centers on sharing what we know (Arnett et al., 2018).

We want to have relationships where we can grow in our understanding of issues and others. To do so, we need to consider how our communication influences our conversations and relationships with the people in our lives. Thus, dialogic ethics prioritizes respect for the other, openness, understanding, and ethical listening as evident in genuine dialogue and technical dialogue (Arnett et al., 2018).

In this activity, you will increase your *knowledge* by describing:

- What is monologue, genuine dialogue, and technical dialogue?
- How is each type of communication evident in the film *Hidden Figures*?
- What is dialogic ethics from the perspective of Martin Buber?

In this activity, you will learn *skills* by investigating:

- What communication practices are required for genuine dialogue?
- How is dialogic ethics part of being an ethical communicator?

In this activity, you will reflect on your own *values* by inquiring:

- What ethical values motivate those who are open to genuine dialogue?

- What ethical values are important to you in communicating with others?

- What obstacles to genuine dialogue need to be removed or guarded against?

In this activity, you will take *action* by:

- Observing when people are committed to building respectful relationships. What kind of actions do they engage in? How do they listen to each other? What is their verbal and nonverbal communication?

- Identifying a relationship in your life where there is I-It communication. What steps could you take to communicate with greater authenticity, openness, and acceptance?

The Activity

In Part I of the activity, complete the recommended reading and analyze scenes from *Hidden Figures* from the perspective of dialogic ethics to gain an understanding of Martin Buber's approach. In Part II, apply your learning to one of your relationships with a friend, coworker, or family member. In Part III, write a reflection paper to synthesize your learning.

© fizkes/Shutterstock.com

Part I: Film Analysis of *Hidden Figures* and Discussion

1. Complete the reading by Arnett et al., (2018) at the end of this chapter.

2. View the following scenes from *Hidden Figures* (based on your instructor's directions):

   a. Mary Jackson meets with Mr. Zielinski [about 1 minute] https://www.youtube.com/watch?v=QJL9TUF95Mo&list=PLDqc8t6GlTabCsNmEsJK90TPvlkOWfIDJ&index=8

    b. Conversation between Mary Jackson and Vivian Mitchell [about 1 minute] https://www.youtube.com/watch?v=00LG8mM01fs

    c. Mary Jackson petitions the court to take advanced courses [2:39 minutes] https://www.youtube.com/watch?v=u8WN9eRdw1U&list=PLneSZhPKfD_IOnvHcTv2Fje4dycgga8rB&index=7

    d. Katherine Johnson explains Euler's Method to her colleagues [about 2 minutes] https://www.youtube.com/watch?v=v-pbGAts_Fg

3. In what ways are the scenes depicting monologue, technical dialogue, and/or genuine dialogue?

4. Meet in small groups to compare responses.

5. Discuss the questions below as a class.

Discussion Questions

1. Based on the scenes from *Hidden Figures*, what type of communication (monologue, technical dialogue, and/or genuine dialogue) is depicted? How does bias impact the type(s) of communication evident in the scene?

2. How do the different types of communication affect the characters' relationships with others in the scene?

3. From the perspective of dialogic ethics, how would you describe the relationship between Mary Jackson and Mr. Zielinski?

4. What types of communication are evident in Mary Jackson's communication with the judge? What was required of them to have this conversation?

Part II: Application

1. Prepare for your reflection paper by identifying an individual with whom you have I-Thou communication. Define I-Thou communication based on the work of Martin Buber. How is your relationship affected by your communication choices?

2. Identify an individual with whom you have I-It communication. Define I-It communication based on Martin Buber. How is your relationship affected by your communication choices?

3. What communication choices could you make with the individual listed in #2 that would invite greater authenticity, openness, and acceptance? (e.g., ethical listening, respect, willingness to learn, etc.)

4. Plan a time to practice your new communication choices with the individual listed in #2 or the person with whom you have I-It communication.

Part III: Reflection Paper

Write a two to three page reflection paper synthesizing your learning about dialogic ethics and how your new communication choices affected your relationship with the person identified in Part II, #2.

1. Provide examples of previous I-It communication with the individual.

2. Discuss the new communication choices you made to invite greater authenticity, openness, and acceptance.

3. What was the result of making new communication choices with the individual?

References

Arnett, R. C., Fritz, J. M. H., & Bell McManus, L. M. (2018). *Communication ethics literacy: Dialogue and difference* (2nd ed.). Kendall Hunt.

Buber, M. (1970). *I and thou*. Simon & Schuster.

YouTube Movies. (2017, January 5). *Hidden figures* [Video]. YouTube. https://www.youtube.com/watch?reload=9&v=U386EMeWo3I

Additional Resources

Neher, W. W., & Sandin, P. J. (2007). *Communicating ethically: Character, duties, consequences, and relationships* (pp. 85–91). Pearson Education, Inc.

Tompkins, P. (2019). *Practicing communication ethics: Development, discernment, and decision making* (2nd ed., pp. 158–164). Routledge.

Listening Otherwise

Chances are you've learned a lot about how to express yourself in your communication classes. Whether it is public speaking, semester presentations, group work, conflict, or the many papers you have been asked to write, a lot of your curriculum is likely learning how to express yourself in a competent, effective, and (in this class) ethical manner. However, one important skill—an important ethical skill, in fact—is often overlooked or assumed, listening.

In learning about communication ethics, we want you to develop skills for listening otherwise. By *otherwise*, we mean the following:

- Listening otherwise "is a sensitivity to the suffering of others that derives from regarding the other's suffering as a concern of mine not because I make some kind of cognitive leap of comprehending the inimitable and infinite connection among all things in the universe, or because of some strategic need I have of you, but because I feel *with* you, ineffably and irrevocably connected but not subsumed" (Lipari, 2009, p. 54).

- "When we bear witness and *listen otherwise,* we listen from a space of unknowing, loss of control, loss of ideas and concept; an opening to what is, not shrinking away, *being* there. . . Bearing witness gives rise to a listening without resorting to what is easy, what I already know, or what we have in common. It means that I listen for and make space for the difficult, the different, and the radically strange" (Lipari, 2009, p. 57).

To sum up, listening *otherwise* challenges us to consider what it means to feel with someone else (empathy) as a listener. Also, consider what it means to bear witness or listen otherwise and its connection to loss of control or being open to uncertainty.

In this activity, you will increase your *knowledge* by considering:

- What is ethical listening/listening otherwise?

- How is ethical listening different from pseudo-listening?

In this activity, you will increase your *skills* by inquiring:

- What skills are needed for active listening, and which ones do you need to develop more?

- What skills are needed for ethical listening (listening otherwise), and which ones do you need to develop more?

- How are the listening skills you use different for face-to-face versus online?

In this activity, you will reflect on your *values* by asking:

- How does ethical listening give primacy to the self or the other?

In this activity, you will take *action* by examining:

- How can you engage in active, ethical listening in your everyday life?

- What specific behaviors and skills can you improve?

The Activity

This activity asks you to engage in active, ethical listening. Have *four* interpersonal conversations where you *really* listen to the other person. Focus only on the other person. Put your phone down (and don't pick it up even if your conversation partner does). Provide appropriate feedback to let the speaker know you are paying attention. Notice how easy or hard it is for you to give others your full attention, especially your own habits of nonlistening and offering not-so-helpful responses. Contact at least *one* person via Zoom, Skype, FaceTime, or other video platform and have at least *two* face-to-face conversations. Write a short response paper and reflect on:

1. How it felt before, during, and after your conversations.

2. How it compares to how you normally listen to others.

3. The kind of responses you received from others.

4. If it was hard or uncomfortable for you and why.

5. The differences between mediated (video call) and face-to-face communication that you observed and felt.

Reference

Lipari, L. (2009). Listening otherwise: The voice of ethics. *International Journal of Listening, 23*(1), 44–59. https://doi.org/10.1080/10904010802591888

Life-Giving Gift of Acknowledgment

To See the Invisible Man

What would life be like if no one acknowledged your existence? Communication ethics scholar Michael Hyde (2006) asks this important question in his book, *The Life-Giving Gift of Acknowledgment*. At first glance, the answer seems simple; life would be lonely or hard. But Hyde's question gets at something more fundamental related to our existence. What makes us alive?

We don't want to be too philosophical here, but it is clear we need air, a beating heart, as well as nutrients and food. If we have all of those things but no one acknowledges us, would we still be alive? Would our lives still have worth and meaning? Think of it this way—if your roommate, friends, family, professors, and co-workers ceased talking to you, would you still exist? Would you still matter?

These are Hyde's questions. While we could spend countless hours trying to figure out what makes us alive, our aim in communication ethics is to figure out the important role communication plays in helping us feel alive, feel included, have meaning, and feel acknowledged. For this activity, you will be watching an old *Twilight Zone* episode that gets at the question of, what would life be like if no one acknowledged your existence?

In this activity, you will increase your *knowledge* by considering:

- What is the difference between acknowledgment and recognition?

- Why is acknowledgment a communicative act?

- Why is acknowledgment life-giving and what does that have to do with communication ethics?

In this activity, you will increase your *skills* by inquiring:

- How do you receive acknowledgment in your everyday life and from whom?

- Who do you most need life-giving acknowledgment from?

- How do you give life-giving acknowledgment, and not mere recognition, to others?

In this activity, you will reflect on your *values* by asking:

- What does it mean to create space for others in your life?

In this activity, you will take *action* by examining:

- How can you give life-giving acknowledgment to others (and not just recognition)?

- What does this look like in terms of observable actions and behaviors?

The Activity

Read the Preface and Chapter 1 of Dr. Hyde's *The Life-Giving Gift of Acknowledgment* (provided in this book), and then watch a *Twilight Episode* from 1986 entitled, *To See the Invisible Man.* Your instructor will provide you links to the episode in three parts on YouTube. Please be aware that the episode is from 1986, so fashion and styles are throwbacks and the production values are low. Try to overlook those qualities and suspend your belief in the social and legal system that is depicted (it's science fiction, so it's not about reality but about exploration of ideas and impacts) and try to focus on the emotion, relationships, and behaviors. Try to put yourself in the shoes of Mitchell. Also note that the episode is based on a short story by Robert Silverberg from 1963 entitled the same, but hard to find.

Once you watch the video, your instructor will either ask you to write a reflection paper or have a discussion. Either way, take notes on what you observe in the film. The best way to approach watching the episode is to identify where you see Dr. Hyde's concepts from the reading illustrated in the episode in preparation for the paper and/or discussion.

References

Hyde, M. J. (2006). *The life-giving gift of acknowledgment: A philosophical and rhetorical inquiry.* Purdue University.

Twilight Zone. (1986, January 31, original air date). To see the invisible man. [Video] YouTube. https://www.youtube.com/watch?v=p0oPwt9n-38

The Virtues of Identity

Who am I? It seems like a simple question, but if you think about it for a moment, you will realize it's actually a difficult question to respond to. Who are you, really? And where did you come from in terms of personality and identity? How did you get to be who you are? And who gave you positive and negative messages about who you are?

There are lots of theories about identity in communication, psychology, sociology, philosophy, political science, and many other disciplines. We are not going to worry about all of those. In this activity, which starts outside of class and involves a guided discussion in class, we will start to reflect not only on who you are, but also how your identity is connected to communication ethics and values.

In this activity, you will increase your *knowledge* by considering:

- How is your identity (your sense of who you are) connected to how others value you?

- What is the social construction of identity?

In this activity, you will increase your *skills* by inquiring:

- How can you identify who you are?

- How can you recognize how society has given you positive and negative messages about who you are?

In this activity, you will reflect on your *values* by asking:

- What identities are valued more in society than others?

- How is what you choose to self-identify as valued or not valued by society? What are those values? What does this say about society?

© iQoncept/Shutterstock.com

In this activity, you will take *action* by examining:

- How can you learn to value yourself and others, despite what society might say or value?

- How can you intervene and support those who might feel marginalized or undervalued by society, not just interpersonally but in terms of social justice or social intervention in a broad way?

The Activity

Complete the worksheet provided here, taking care to follow instructions as they are written. Additional instruction will be provided by your instructor, including a possible reflection paper or post for an online discussion board based on step 3.

Identity and Values Worksheet

NAME: _____

Instructions

1. Write your name above. Now, think about how you see yourself and how others see you.

2. On the chart below, outline the eight most salient identities that make up who you are. These could be group or role affiliations. Consider the following list (but you are by no means limited to it): family role, friendship, religion, race, workplace role, volunteer role(s), physical appearance, gender identity, gender expression, age, economic class, disability, ethnic group, country of origin, sexual orientation, state of physical or mental health, school affiliation, political belief/ideology, geographic location of home, neighborhood, language, and hobbies/pastimes. Your identity markers do not have to be ranked, but could be.

3. As directed by your instructor, be prepared to share your identities with others in class. Consider: Why did you self-identify in that way? What identities did you consider and not include? Why did you choose these identities? What are some sources of pride with one or more of the identities you wrote down? What is an area of accomplishment or a meaningful relationship associated with a specific identity? ***Importantly, how do you express that identity?***

4. In Column #2, for each identity, ask what makes that identity good or bad. For instance, you might say a good student means studying hard or a bad student is one who does not go to class. Complete *two things* that make that identity good and *two things* that make that identity bad for each of your identities. Be prepared to share in pairs or a small group.

5. After completing Column #2, complete Column #3 by reflecting on where you heard the different judgments and messages you identified in Column #2. For instance, you may notice that your parents and teachers told you that good students are those who study hard because they are the ones who get good grades, and that bad students do not get good grades because they do not go to class. The emphasis here is on what/who is the source of the messages in Column #2 in your life. This may be family, friends, teachers, church figures, television shows, social media, news, magazines, etc. Be specific.

Column #1: My Identities	Column #2: Good and Bad	Column #3: Source
Ex: Professor	• Professors are nerdy and geeky (bad) • Professors are super smart and deserve respect	• My brother always called me a geek and nerd when I studied in high school rather than going out to socialize. • I always thought it was cool to see "Dr. _____" on the morning news shows discussing the latest news topic.
1.		
2.		
3.		
4.		
5.		

6.		
7.		
8.		

Reciprocity, Fairness, and Cooperation

If you worked at your job, but did not get paid, how would you feel? Or if you loaned someone money and he or she never paid you back, what feelings do you think would emerge? Have you ever heard young children say that because someone else was playing with their toys that it wasn't fair! Chances are you would feel like you were owed something if you didn't get paid or didn't get the money back you loaned out. You would feel, like those children, that it wasn't fair! If so, you were concerned about the desire for *reciprocity*.

Reciprocity is simply defined as exchanging things for mutual benefit. This can be positive—you buy a cup of coffee for a friend and the next time your friend buys you the cup of coffee. It can also be negative where you punish others for violating this norm. For example, if your friend didn't get you a gift for Christmas, you might decide not to reciprocate with a gift in response.

Reciprocity gets complex though. For example, waiting in line is actually an example of reciprocity. If you wait in line and someone cuts in front of you, they are violating reciprocity, which is explained in the norm of wait your turn. When someone cuts, it feels unfair and you or others may ask the individual to go to the back of the line or even leave. A negative form of reciprocity is war and violence. When one country attacks another, the country that was attacked feels a need to respond in order for things to feel fair.

At the heart of reciprocity is fairness, and we often evaluate fairness in terms of an exchange of benefits. If you work, you expect fair pay. If you help your friend move out of an apartment, you expect a reward in return of some kind. Of course, that reciprocal exchange varies: you want a paycheck for your work, but you might settle for a thank you or a pizza from your friend. When this expectation is violated, it feels unfair. You might even say unjust. Indeed, reciprocity is the foundation of justice. When someone commits a crime, justice is about the criminal paying their dues to society, whether it be a fine, community service, or jail time.

Reciprocity's positive side is called cooperation. On a team, everyone has to play a role in order for the team to be successful. When everyone plays their role, there is cooperation that can lead not only to success, but also long-term survival. Trade between countries is an excellent example because when two nations are involved in a mutually beneficial relationship, both are working toward long-term survival. In fact, many scholars believe reciprocity is hardwired into the human species because in order to survive as a species and as individuals, we must cooperate with one another.

The Golden Rule is an excellent example of reciprocity: Do unto others as you would have them do unto you. In other words, if you treat people the way you want to be treated, everything is fair. But when this rule, and reciprocity in general, is violated we feel like we are owed something. Reciprocity helps us see that we live in a network of obligations, where we owe and are owed many things, from expressions of gratitude to a paycheck to justice to international trade.

In this activity, you will increase your *knowledge* by considering:

- What is reciprocity?
- What are different forms of reciprocity throughout history and across cultures?
- How is reciprocity and cooperation hardwired into being human and necessary for survival?
- What does reciprocity have to do with what we feel we owe to others and others owe to us?

In this activity, you will increase your *skills* by inquiring:

- How can I recognize when I need to apply reciprocity?
- How can I recognize when reciprocity may not be an appropriate ethical norm to follow?

In this activity, you will reflect on your *values* by asking:

- How is fairness the basis for many of my actions and decisions in my life and in the lives of others around me?
- How is fairness the basis for justice?
- How is reciprocity one of the strongest norms I live by?

In this activity, you will take *action* by examining:

- How do I recognize when reciprocity is the basis for my or others' actions?
- How do I engage in reciprocity for others, especially those close to me?
- What kinds of action can I take when I feel I've been denied reciprocity?

The Activity

This activity is designed to get you thinking about reciprocity in your life in small, everyday ways. Likely, your instructor will use this activity as preparation for a discussion. The activity is simple: Take a blank piece of paper or a blank word processor and write out as many social transactions as you can remember from the time you woke up (or yesterday if you're trying to finish this activity early before class). For example, did you say hello to your roommate? Did you let someone into traffic to be nice? Did you clean up your dishes before you left your apartment? Did you purchase something at a store?

After doing that, identify if reciprocity was involved and if so, how. This will take on two forms—one positive and the other negative. The positive is where you promoted cooperation; the negative is where you felt like you or someone else violated the norm of reciprocity. You might set up two columns—one that describes the social transaction and the other that describes the form of reciprocity. See the following example.

Social transaction from my day	Form of reciprocity
Said good morning to roommate	*Promoting positive relationships between roommates*
Let someone go in front of me in traffic	*Promoting cooperation for more efficient traffic flow*
Said hello to my ex	*My ex did not respond; I felt upset and like I was owed at least a hello. We can still be civil!*
Dropped leftover change in a donation box for the homeless	*Helping others means others feel better and less people living on the street.*
Kept texting on my phone even when my classmate was trying to organize our group	*I messed up by not responding to my peer, I didn't respond in kind.*

Pay attention to what your instructor asks of you; you may be asked to write a short reflection paper based on your table.

The Ethical Inevitability of Conflict

We live in a world where conflict is an inescapable feature of life, in families, communities, workplaces, and global concerns. Understanding why conflict arises is critical to knowing how to respond to others and manage the situation as best as you can (Kellett & Dalton, 2001; Wilmont & Hocker, 2007). Though we often situate conflict as bad, hard, and something to avoid, there is much to learn from analyzing why, how, and in what ways conflict erupts or grows. You might ask, what are the differences in values that are evident among the different parties to the conflict? By reflecting on the situation, the communication, and the values embedded in the conflict, you will be better able to navigate the inevitable tensions of life, be they big or small. Arnett, Bell McManus, and McKendree (2018) articulate the importance of studying conflict through an ethical lens stating that it is our "dissimilar ethical standpoints that generate conflict" (p. 1). There is a great deal to learn from our differences that are often closely connected to social, economic, cultural, and historical experiences. While conflict may be inevitable, you have the opportunity to influence the outcome through critical thinking and reflection.

A practical application of a conflict situation focuses on the important nature of dialogue. As we engage in dialogic negotiations, the relational space between us (Buber, 2002) allows us to analyze and reflect upon our communicative actions (Pearce & Pearce, 2004). One of the seminal works in conflict that allows us to evaluate our communicative actions comes from the work of Thomas and Kilmann (1974) who identified five conflict styles that describe how most people handle conflict situations. The first style is *avoiding* where people intentionally circumvent the conflict situation. The second is *accommodating* which focuses on appealing to others. The third style is *competing* that allows for the constant power struggle of winning the conflict. The fourth style is *compromising* that focuses on the give-and-take nature of negotiating a conflict. The fifth and final style is *collaborating* where creative alternatives are proposed to allow for mutual satisfaction. As you participate in this activity, reflect on your experiences with different conflict situations and try to recognize which of the five conflict styles you have used.

In this activity, you'll increase your *knowledge* by thinking about:

- How do past conflict situations act as learning experiences?

- How do past experiences dealing with conflict influence your current conflict situations?

- What are the various ways that people respond to conflict?

You'll have the opportunity to learn *skills* by considering:

- How do you approach conflict situations in various contexts?

- What style of conflict (accommodating, avoiding, competing, compromising, or collaborating) do you gravitate toward in conflict situations?

- How can dialogue help move a conflict to a deeper learning experience?

You can consider your own *values* and that of others by asking:

- What matters are significant enough for you to have a conflict over?

- What issues personally and professionally create conflict situations?

Putting what you learn into *action* means:

- What different choices can you make upon reflecting on how you've handled past conflict situations?

- What goals can you establish for yourself in a specific conflict situation to generate more productive results?

Activity

In the box draw a picture of conflict.

Discussion

- What does conflict look like to you? Why?

- What are the similarities and differences in the various class pictures?

After analyzing the drawings watch the "After Dinner Conflict Scene" found in the movie *The Break Up* (2006), https://www.youtube.com/watch?v=_bqhVqTuFO4

Discuss the following questions

- What was the conflict about?

- How was the conflict handled on both sides?

- How could this conflict be managed differently?

- What are the ethical assumptions associated with this particular conflict?

References

Arnett, R. C., Bell McManus, L. M., & McKendree A. G. (2018). *Conflict between persons: The origins of leadership* (2nd ed.). Kendall Hunt.

Arnett, R. C., Fritz, J. H., & Bell McManus, L. M. (2018). *Communication ethics literacy: Dialogue and difference* (2nd ed.). Kendall Hunt.

Buber, M. (2002). *Between man and man* (R. G. Smith Trans.). Macmillan (Original work published in 1947).

Fisher, R., Ury, W., & Patton, B. (1991). *Getting to yes: Negotiating agreement without giving in* (2nd ed.). Penguin Books.

Kellett, P. M., & Dalton, D. G. (2001). *Managing conflict in a negotiated world: A narrative approach to achieving dialogue and change.* Sage Publications.

Pearce, W. B., & Pearce, K. A. (2004). Taking a communication perspective on dialogue. In R. Anderson, L. A. Baxter, & K. N. Cissna (Eds.), *Dialogue: Theorizing difference in communication studies* (pp. 39–56). Sage.

The Break-Up. (2006). [Video]. YouTube. https://www.youtube.com/watch?v=_bqhVqTuFO4

Thomas, K. W., & Kilmann, R. H. (1974). *Thomas-Kilmann conflict mode instrument.* Xicom, Inc.

Wilmont, W. W., & Hocker, J. L. (2007). *Interpersonal conflict* (7th ed.). McGraw-Hill.

Reading: *Communication Ethics Literacy: Dialogue and Difference* by Ronald C. Arnett, Janie M. Harden Fritz, and Leeanne M. Bell McManus

Martin Buber

Buber suggests that dialogue lives outside of demand and is not "normative" in day-to-day interaction. Dialogue is not "the" way to communicate or a common mode of communication. Dialogue is only one way to communicate with another. Buber reminds us about the relational importance of monologue that seeks to tell with primary focus on what one already knows; of technical dialogue that seeks to encourage the exchange of information; and genuine dialogue, where insight emerges between persons, insight that belongs to neither one nor the other. Dialogic ethics assumes the importance of technical dialogue *and* genuine dialogue, considering the former what we can engage regularly and the latter a human gift that brings insight and meaning beyond expectation. Dialogue is both the learning of technical dialogue and the gift giving dialogue that emerges as a byproduct, not planned or engineered, but ever so responsive to the unexpected moments of communicative encounter.

Deborah Eicher-Catt (2017) emphasizes the importance of Maggie Jackson's book, *Distracted: The Erosion of Attention and the Coming Dark Age* (2008). Her point is that the world, understood as a tool, or something simply to be used, moves our attention quickly from one issue to another. Our engagement with distinctiveness and uniqueness falls to the wayside as we construct an increasingly disenchanted world. Such a place is void of the revelatory and the unexpected, the "ah ha" of everyday meeting of others. She points to enchantment as the byproduct of human dialogue, ever attentive to difference between persons and the revelatory that propels surprise, appreciation, and wonder.

Contrary to its common denouncement, monologue has an important place in communicative life. There are times when the Other should "tell" us information; we simply take notes and listen. One of our colleagues uses lecture as the primary way of engaging learning in his classroom. We are supportive of him as he reminds students and us that monologue is a healthy and needed part of life. Ironically, to refuse ever to be part of a monologic environment makes dialogue impossible, turning dialogue into a demand. If one takes music lessons, a skilled teacher may go on and on about music theory as if there were no one else in the room. Yet, much learning emerges—notes, memory, and listening take the telling and turn it into learning. To demand that each exchange be dialogic is to overvalue one's own significance. Yet, when this same teacher works with young people, there is a reaching out that encourages their playing and practice. He begins not with theory, but with asking about their week and looking over the practice schedule that he asks them to record. He then asks them to evaluate how well they can play a given piece of music, connecting their evaluation to practice time. He works with them gently, with the music connected to practice. He works each week to link quality of performance with time spent on a given piece of music. Watching him work with a younger performer illustrates technical dialogue at work, and there is joy in watching the smile on the teacher's face in the "telling" to his older student, bringing monologue into the conversation as a teacher and musician. If one wants to learn, then valuing monologue is a beginning. If we do not value another's telling, we move to dialogue upon demand, and dialogue, by definition, resists the demand that communicative life meet "my" standards. For a more complete understanding of dialogue, see the recent work of Ronald C. Arnett (2012b, 2014, 2015).

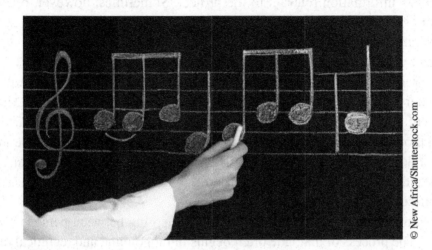

Buber moves the conversation to discuss the interplay of images in a relational exchange, involving six tacit communicative exchanges, including (1) my image of myself, (2) my image of the Other, (3) my image of the Other's image of me, (4) the Other's image of the Other, (5) the Other's image of me, and (6) the Others image of my image of the Other, illustrating different perspectives on self and other. When image no longer dominates, dialogue is possible. Yet, the very effort to "try to be in dialogue" makes it impossible, keeping one's image of oneself as a "dialogic person" more important than the dialogue itself. Much of life is more akin to technical dialogue than to "true" dialogue, attending to complexity of images of self and other in informative exchange. Theories that seek to bring these images together thrive. For instance, John Stewart (2011) discusses a transactional model of communication that integrates these differing images. The insight of Pearce and Cronen (1980) in their depiction of the coordinated management of meaning reminds us of the ongoing complexity of bringing diverse perspectives together. The still ground-breaking work of George Herbert Mead (1962) in symbolic interaction theory details differing images of "I" and "me" (p. 173–178), with the latter more attentive to image construction. Mead's work is particularly important; he considers communicative interaction the primary shaper of the self-concept.

In essence, the six dimensions of image summarized by Buber point to a reality sustained by one theory after another. Images matter. One must negotiate images without confusing the notion of image with the engagement of human dialogue. A dialogic ethic begins with the assumption that one cannot take on the image of a "dialogic person," a "dialogue maker," or a "dialogue broker." To do so is to move dialogue into a disguise, the image of being dialogic. Much of life requires negotiating of images more akin to monologue or, at best, technical dialogue.

Suppose that Madison's and Terrell's instructor has just assigned them to the same group for a class project related to service learning. They do not know each other at all; their initial encounters consist of small talk and opinions about the project, which involves interviewing children in after-school programs to determine learning needs. Each student works with images of self and others, negotiating images that present themselves as concerned, collaborative group members. Terrell, however, does not want to appear overly eager to excel; he presents a different image.

Over the course of the term, Madison and Terrell engage in a great deal of technical dialogue focused on information relevant to the project. Sometimes, however, one of them will reveal something that generates a response in the other. For example, Terrell once remarked, "I am glad we are doing this project. I wish I had had this type of support in an after-school program when I was growing up." Madison then asks questions about Terrell's life; the two are surprised to discover that an entire hour has passed, and in the process, several new insights about each other and the project emerged. Looking back on their experience, Madison states, "It is funny, but we never intended to get into such a deep discussion. I learned more about Terrell than I thought I would just working on this project. At first, I thought he just wanted to get the project done to fulfill the course requirement, but now I see that it means a lot to him. I also understand this project differently than I did at first, and that would not have happened without our discussions."

Images begin the conversation, and information emerging between persons offers an unexpected ending. The process of dialogue often begins in monologue and technical dialogue, only to surprise us with its emergence when least expected. If we move the conversation about images and dialogue to dialogue and difference, we open the discussion to the dialogic work of Gadamer, who reminds us of the importance of bias to human communication and learning. Dialogue begins with difference.

References

Arnett, R. C. (2012b). The fulcrum point of dialogue: Monologue, worldview, and acknowledgment. *American Journal of Semiotics, 28,* 105–127.

Arnett, R. C. (2014). Civic dialogue: Attending to locality and recovering monologue. *Journal of Dialogue Studies, 2*(2), 71–92.

Arnett, R. C. (2015). The dialogic necessity: Acknowledging and engaging monologue. *Ohio Communication Journal, 53,* 1–10.

Eicher-Catt, D. (2017). A prelude to a semioethics of dialogue. *Language and Dialogue, 7,* 100–119.

Mead, G. H. (1962). *Mind, self, and society: From the standpoint of a social behaviorist.* C. W. Morris (Ed.). Chicago, IL: University of Chicago Press.

Pearce, W. B., & Cronen, V. E. (1980). *Communication, action, and meaning: The creation of social realities.* New York, NY: Praeger.

Stewart, J. R. (2011). *Bridges not walls: A book about interpersonal communication* (11th ed.). Columbus, OH: McGraw-Hill.

Reading: *The Life-Giving Gift of Acknowledgment* by Michael J. Hyde

What would life be like if no one *acknowledged* your existence? The question confronts one with the possibility of being isolated, marginalized, ignored, and forgotten by others. The unacknowledged find themselves in an "out-of-the-way" place where it is hard for human beings, given their social instinct, to feel at home. The suffering that can accompany this way of being-in-the-world is known to bring about fear, anxiety, sadness, anger, and sometimes even death in the form of suicide or retaliation against those who are rightly or wrongly accused of making one's life so lonely, miserable, and unbearable.

Acknowledgment provides an opening out of such a distressful situation, for the act of acknowledging is a communicative behavior that grants attention to others and thereby makes room for them in our lives. With this added living space comes the opportunity for a new beginning, a "second chance" whereby one might improve his or her lot in life. There is hope to be found with this transformation of space and time as people of conscience opt to go out of their way to make us feel wanted and needed, to praise our presence and actions, and thus to acknowledge the worthiness of our existence. Offering positive acknowledgment is a moral thing to do.

Granted, such acknowledgment may embarrass us, and it might even make us feel guilty if we know that our presence and actions have something deceitful about them or, at least in our humble opinion, are not really that great. But generally speaking, positive acknowledgment makes us feel good, as it recognizes something about our being that is felt by others to be worthy of praise and perhaps even remembrance after we are gone. Indeed, have you ever thought about your own death, your funeral, and who might show up to pay their respects? And when thinking about this last matter, have you ever become upset with those people who you believe should have attended the ceremony but did not? Even when we have passed to the most out-of-the-way place there is, we still crave the goodness of positive acknowledgment—the way it brings us to mind and thus, in a sense, keeps us "alive." Following Ernest Becker, then, one might say that acknowledgment provides a way to satisfy a human being's "urge to immortality"—an urge that "is not a simple reflex of the death anxiety but a reaching out by one's whole being toward life . . . , a reaching-out for a plenitude of meaning. . . . It seems that the life force reaches naturally even beyond the earth itself, which is one reason why man has always placed God in the heavens."

Of course, not all acknowledgment that comes our way is positive. For example, hearing someone say "Looking good" to you in a certain situation may be understood correctly as a compliment. In a different situation, however, these same words, coming from someone with whom you have never gotten along, might also be legitimately heard as a sarcasm, a slight, an articulation whose tone of voice speaks ridicule, disrespect, and dislike. Such negative acknowledgment is also at work whenever we call people "stupid" or "worthless," thereby opening and exposing them to the further ridicule of others. Like its opposite, negative acknowledgment creates a place for being noticed. But the space created here, even if it is made with the best of intentions—as when a parent, trying to provide careful guidance, scolds a child for being "naughty"—more often than not makes us feel bad.

From *The Life-Giving Gift of Acknowledgment*. Reproduced with permission of Purdue University Press.

Acknowledgment is a significant and powerful form of behavior, one that can bring joy to a person's heart and also drive a stake through it. Acknowledgment functions as both a life-giving gift and a life-draining force. Moving from its positive to negative form and then to a state of no acknowledgment at all, we find ourselves in a place that is hard-pressed to support life because it is so barren of the nourishment provided by the caring concern of others. Institutionalized forms of negative acknowledgment such as racism, sexism, and ageism expose people to this fate. Certain rituals of culture, on the other hand, are meant to protect us from it. Proper decorum dictates, for example, that we say "hello" and "goodbye" to people so that they feel noticed; that we make them feel important and respected by simply holding open a door and saying "after you"; or that we send them a birthday or condolence card to assure them that, at a moment of great joy or great distress, they are in our thoughts and perhaps our prayers. The presence of people in need of acknowledgment sounds a call of conscience: "Where art thou?" Good manners encourage us to say, "Here I am!" Knowing or at least believing that this response truly "comes from the heart," others are likely to feel better than if they know or believe that what they are receiving is mostly some ritualized behavior steeped in the shallows of unthinking habit rather than in the depths of genuine care.

The difference in "feeling" being noted here corresponds to what I take to be the essential difference that exists between the phenomena of acknowledgment and simple "recognition." People often speak of these two phenomena as if they were one in the same. For the purposes of the current project, however, their difference must be kept in mind. Consider the following example, which describes an interaction that I suspect most readers have had in their lives.

Acknowledgment and Recognition

While walking down the street, John notices a person approaching him whom he recognizes to be an old acquaintance, Mary. She notices and recognizes John, too, and they greet each other with "heys!" and some gentle pats on the back. "Long time no see. How've you been? What's going on?" asks Mary. John's reply is simple: "Great! Nothing much. I am just heading to my office." John then asks Mary the same questions as a way of being polite, hoping that her reply will be equally economical, for John has many things to do today at the office and he is not much in the mood for conversation.

Not having made this point clear to Mary, however, John begins to hear answers that he senses might be too involved and time-consuming for his immediate purposes. John displays some non-verbal cues (looking away from Mary's face and shifting his body from side to side) that, as far as he is concerned, are commonsensical enough to be read as a clear but still polite indication that "now is not the time to get into all of this stuff." For whatever reason, however, Mary is determined to share with John what is on her mind, and, therefore, she disregards or perhaps remains oblivious to his cues. After another fifteen seconds of "listening" to her speak, John feels compelled to interrupt at an "appropriate" moment with a not entirely truthful excuse: "Mary, I'm sorry, but I have an appointment that I can't miss. How about if I try to give you a call later this week and maybe we can arrange to do lunch." "Of course," says Mary. "I look forward to hearing from you. Really, let's get together."

Mary is being genuine with this last request. She is seeking more than the recognition that John has given her so far; she is looking forward to the added space and time, the openness, that comes with John's acknowledgment of her and that provides a "dwelling place" (*ethos*) for developing a more caring conversation. This *ethos* of acknowledgment establishes an environment wherein people can take the time to "know together" (*con-scientia*) some topic of interest and, in the process, perhaps gain a more authentic understanding of those who are willing to contribute to its development. Recognition is only a preliminary step in this process of attuning one's consciousness toward another and his or her expression of a topic in order to facilitate the development of such existential knowledge and personal understanding. Acknowledgment requires a sustained openness to others even if, at times, things become boring or troublesome.

Such openness is what Mary wanted and was willing to give. John, on the other hand, opted to keep the relationship in a state of simple recognition—a state that at least gives the impression that one is being noticed and that genuine acknowledgment is thus a possibility. If this possibility is negated by John's decision not to call Mary later in the week, then she has evidence that might rightly lead her to think that the extent of John's acknowledgment of her was more of a ruse than anything else. "Where art thou?" John offers no "Here I am!"

In his related investigations of the nature of skepticism and the dynamics of tragedy, Stanley Cavell teaches that "the alternative to my acknowledgment of the other is not my ignorance of him but my avoidance of him, call it my denial of him." Moreover, Cavell contends that acknowledgment, and not just mere recognition, is "something owed another simply as a human being, the failure of which reveals the failure of one's own humanity." I agree with both of these statements. John's behavior is an affront to Mary's being. He owes her an apology: "I know I was wrong not to get back in touch with you, Mary." As Cavell points out, to say "I know" in this case "is to admit, confess, *acknowledge*." With his apology John *opens* himself to Mary, *reveals* that he *knows* himself to be guilty of a wrongdoing that most likely was harmful to her well-being, and thereby acknowledges and *affirms* Mary's existence—"Here I am!"—by granting her the time and space, the dwelling place, that is needed for her to offer an "appropriate" response. Following Cavell, one could now describe John as a person who has "shown his humanity."

Mary, of course, will be the judge of this display of humanity as she decides whether John's apology does in fact "come from the heart," whether he is truly sorry, and whether this time he is, indeed, offering her the life-giving gift of acknowledgment and not just another mere moment of manipulating recognition. For Cavell, our everyday understanding of the world stabilizes itself in our "agreements of judgment" about the authenticity of acknowledgments that are offered by ourselves and others for the purpose of giving meaningful and moral direction to all that we say and do. In other words, the stability of any given symbolic order presupposes a process of people working together to acknowledge their acknowledgments and to agree on or question the "truth" of these acknowledgments. Ludwig Wittgenstein, whose philosophical investigations of language use informs Cavell's take on the matter, puts it this way: "Knowledge is in the end based on acknowledgments." Cavell writes in the hope that readers will acknowledge the sensibleness of his stance on acknowledgment and thereby agree with his earlier quoted claim that, in the name of humanity, acknowledgment is "something owed another simply as a human being."

Indeed, acknowledgment *is* a life-giving gift; it makes possible the moral development of recognition. This different way of stating the claim is significant for my purposes. Throughout this book I attempt to go further than Cavell in acknowledging the scope and function of acknowledgment by focusing on its lifegiving capacity—a capacity that enables us to be open to the world of people, places, and things such that we can "admit" (Middle English: *acknow*) its wonders into our minds and then "admit" (Middle English: *knowlechen*) to others the understanding we have gained and that we believe is worth sharing. *The project is undertaken with the belief that the phenomenon of acknowledgment ought to warrant careful and continual attention from anyone whose life would suffer without it.* This belief is certainly affirmed, for example, by social scientific research dealing with the therapeutic effects of "supportive communication" in healthcare, family, and organizational settings. I, too, am interested in such effects, although my appreciation of them follows from a phenomenological understanding of acknowledgment. What is revealed here about the phenomenon is thus directed toward certain of its essential (ontological) aspects whose existential robustness is too often left unacknowledged and thus unappreciated when the measurement of effects is given priority in the scientific study of the phenomenon. I have pointed to certain of these aspects in the discussion so far. They include such things as time, space, openness, emotion, discourse, conscience, and the alterity or otherness of others that necessarily is a part of social existence. All of these things and acknowledgment go hand in hand; the "evolution" of the relationship is essential to the communal spirit and moral well-being of humankind.

In developing this last point throughout the book, I, at the same time, will be making an argument for the importance of people becoming ever more "competent" in the practice of acknowledgment. I thus must be clear at the outset about my understanding and use of this term.

Acknowledgment and Rhetoric

Beginning at least with the ancient Sophists, the study and the teaching of such competence has been associated with the "art of rhetoric"—a practical art that, once Socrates, Plato, Aristotle, and Cicero all had their say about it, was appreciated as a type of "know how," a complex competence that gives expression to our ability to inspire critical judgment about contestable matters, to encourage collaborative deliberation, and to be persuasive. Rhetoric is at work whenever language is being employed to *open* people to ideas, positions, and circumstances that, if rightly understood, stand a better than even chance of getting people to think and act wisely. Orators are forever attempting to create these openings, for this is how they maximize the chance that the members of some audience will take an interest in what is being said. Neither persuasion nor collaborative deliberation can take place without the formation of this joint interest. "We interest a man by dealing with his interests," writes Kenneth Burke. Indeed, and acknowledgment happens as such dealing takes place. The "good" speaker is always seeking acknowledgment from some audience whose "good" members are also waiting for the speaker to acknowledge their interests in some meaningful way. In short, rhetorical competence has a significant role to play in providing places (openings) where a life-giving gift can be received.

For those who are in the habit of thinking about rhetoric in only a pejorative way—that is, for example, as it was used by John to deceive Mary—the present project may seem to be, to say the least, a bit wrongheaded. I hope, however, that when all is said and done I am not merely understood to be claiming something akin to what Gorgias supposedly once said about the power and importance of rhetoric when defending his "craft" to Socrates: ". . . if a rhetorician and a doctor visited any city you like to name and they had to contend in argument before the Assembly or any other gathering as to which of the two should be chosen as doctor, the doctor would be nowhere, but the man who could speak would be chosen, if he so wished." Such a claim, to be sure, is sophistry gone too far, an unfortunate burst of egoism coming from a theorist, teacher, and practitioner of an art that was then, and still is now, in need of positive acknowledgment from its detractors. The art of rhetoric is fated to admit a defensive posture as long as its material is used in unethical ways and for immoral purposes. Still, I think it warrants praise for its potential for creating places where acknowledgment can happen and flourish.

Gorgias was a master when it came to putting to use this inventive capacity of rhetoric. And so was Abraham Lincoln, although, unlike Gorgias, Lincoln did believe in the importance and legitimacy of seeking, finding, and articulating the truth about matters of importance. Consider, for example, his Gettysburg Address, a short piece of oratory whose 272 words are now widely recognized as having "remade America." Lincoln performed this rhetorical feat by creating a particular opening where his present and ever-growing future audience could recognize and know together the honorable deeds of others. The opening that is created in the Address allows for the appropriate amount of aesthetic distance to form between Lincoln's subject matter and his audience. Commenting on this specific artistic and rhetorical happening, Richard Weaver notes: "If one sees an object from too close, one sees only its irregularities and protuberances. To see an object right or to see it as a whole, one has to have a proportioned distance from it." Weaver then goes on to claim that "at Gettysburg, Lincoln spoke in terms so 'generic' that it is almost impossible to show that the speech is not a eulogy of the men in grey as well as the men in blue, inasmuch as both made up 'those who struggled here.' Lincoln's faculty of transcending an occasion [like Gettysburg] is in fact only this ability to view it [rhetorically] from the right distance, or to be wisely generic about it."

I agree with Weaver's assessment of Lincoln. Moreover, like Weaver and many others, I think of Lincoln as exemplifying what the orator is obligated to be: "the ethical teacher of society," or what Weaver elsewhere describes as a "doctor of culture." Lincoln was and remains such a person because he possessed the requisite rhetorical competence needed to create the openings of places where the "truth" and thus the awesomeness of objects, events, and people could be rightly acknowledged. This is the standard of competence that I will have in mind when discussing the particular communicative behavior in question here. Be it positive or negative, the genuine expression of acknowledgment must always make at least some use of the human capacity of rhetorical competence. That this fact of life has long been and will continue to be taken advantage of by people with evil intentions defines yet another good reason for investigating the nature of acknowledgment—what it is and how it functions. I hope to show that genuine acknowledgment is informed by an ontological impulse that points people in the direction of "the good and the just." I also hope to make clear how rhetoric that fails to serve this end is not being true to its essence, which consists of being a tool for acknowledgment— something that is necessary for the well-being of humankind.

Acknowledgment, Creation, and Hope

The story I have to tell about the ontological and rhetorical workings of acknowledgment speaks of creation and hope. Acknowledgment is a moral act; it functions to transform space and time, to *create* openings wherein people can dwell, deliberate, and know together what is right, good, just, and truthful. Acknowledgment thereby grants people *hope*, the opportunity for a new beginning, a second chance, whereby they might improve their lot in life. In developing these points throughout the remaining chapters of this book, I will thus be addressing the concerns of and offering a critical response to those who, like the literary theorist, critic, and philosopher George Steiner, contend that

> The twentieth century has put in doubt the theological, the philosophical and the political-material insurance for hope. It queries the rationale and credibility of future tenses. . . .Who except fundamentalists now awaits the actual coming of a Messiah? Who except literalists of a lost communism or anarcho-socialist Arcadia now awaits the actual re-birth of history? . . . Grammars of nihilism flicker . . . on the horizon.

Steiner takes "grammar" to mean "the articulate organization of perception, reflections and experience, the nerve structure of consciousness when it communicates with itself and with others" (*GC* 6). The "grammar" of the Judeo-Christian theory of creation provides the most well-known and hopeful world-view. Steiner emphasizes, however, that this grammar has been called into question by the "violence, oppression, economic enslavement and social irrationality" that have transpired over the last century. Moreover, he notes, the "grammar" of science offered by the "new cosmologies regard 'creation' as being ambiguous, mythological, and even taboo. To ask what preceded the Big Bang and the primal nanoseconds of the compaction and expansion of our universe is, we are instructed, to talk gibberish" (*GC* 336). Steiner also identifies the "postmodern" literary and philosophical projects of "deconstruction" that seek direction from such thinkers as Jacques Derrida to be additional sources of discontent when it comes to an appreciation of "origins" and "beginnings" made possible by the presence of some Supreme reason or by the genius of creative artists. "Deconstruction, in today's critical theories of meaning, is . . . an 'un-building' of those classical models of meaning which assumed the existence of a precedent *auctoritas*, of a master-builder. There are in Derridean deconstruction neither 'fathers' nor beginnings" (*GC* 22–23).

Of these two grammars of nihilism, Steiner objects most strenuously to the first. Near the end of his work he thus does not hesitate to claim that

> Both elementary logic and common sense should tell us that [science's] ruling [about the "nothingness" that came before the Big Bang] is arrogant bluff. The simple fact that we can phrase the question, that we can engage it with normal thought processes, gives it meaning and legitimacy. The postulate of unquestionable ("not to be questioned") nothingness and intemporality now made dogma by astrophysicists is as arbitrary, is in many regards more of a mystique, than are creation narratives in Genesis and elsewhere. The reasoned intuition of a coming into being which we do not understand, but whose efficacy suggests itself via the analogies of human creativity [as seen in the arts, for example], has lost none of its challenge. . . . The God-hypothesis will not be mocked without cost. (*GC* 336)

Steiner wrote his book to substantiate and dramatize this last point—one that is phrased in an especially self-revealing way in the book's final sentences: "We have long been, I believe that we still are, guests of creation. We owe to our host the courtesy of questioning" (*GC* 338).

This assertion harkens back in a challenging, albeit indirect, manner to the book's first sentence, which records the author's assessment of our present-day postmodern condition: "We have no more beginnings" (*GC* 2). The assertion also reflects Steiner's Judaic heritage and its teachings on the importance of hearing and responding to "the Word" uttered "in the beginning." Steiner puts it this way:

> Speech demands a listener and, if possible, a respondent. To whom does God say, in Genesis I, 26, *naase adam*—"let us make man"? To His own solitude at the very hour in which that solitude is to be broken by the creation of man-the-listener, of man-the-respondent and gainsayer. In echoing turn, human speech declares its origins in transcendent dialogue. We speak because we were called upon to answer; language is, in the root sense, a "vocation." (*GC* 34)

Caught up in this vocation, human beings show themselves to be, among other things, the questioning animal—"*homo quaerens*, the animal that asks and asks" and, in so doing, affirms the presence, the "otherness," of what is "out there," something that needs to be understood for the purpose of making the world as meaningful and as moral as possible (*GC* 20). The "God-hypothesis"—which comes to us from religion and which, as Steiner sees it, is granted feasibility in the wondrous, creative accomplishments of human beings—treats this otherness with the highest reverence.

> [The great] poet, playwright, or novelist names his characters as Adam names the animals around him; in either case, nomination entails both truth and "real" existence. The successful dramatist or story-teller or painter is "God" in large miniature. He or she ushers into the world agents out of the imaginary, out of some dust of pre-existence, whose subsequent fate, whose freedom of action can, precisely as in the mystery of free will accorded by God to His creations, challenge the maker. (*GC* 173)

As he continues to develop this analogy between religion and aesthetics, Steiner also would have us grant that, as is the case with "the Word,"

> It is the production and reception of works of art, in the widest sense, which enables us to share in the experiencing of duration, of time unbounded. Without the arts, the human psyche would stand naked in the face of personal extinction. Wherein would lie the logic of madness and despair. It is (again together with transcendent religious faith and, often, in a certain relation to it) *poiesis* which authorizes the unreason of hope.
>
> In that immensely significant sense, the arts are more indispensable to men and women than even the best of science and technology (innumerable societies have long endured without these). Creativity in the arts and in philosophic proposal is, in respect of the survival of consciousness, of another order than is invention in the sciences. We are an animal whose life-breath is that of spoken, painted, sculptured, sung dreams. . . . Truth is, indeed, with the equation and the axiom; but it is a lesser truth. (*GC* 259)

As *homo quaerens,* who perhaps has yet to abandon all hope for a better world, Steiner would have us keep in mind and once again learn to appreciate the greater truth—if not for God's sake then at least for the sake of the arts and humanities and whatever is left of their "grammars of creation."

The story I have to tell about the ontological and rhetorical workings of acknowledgment contains its own grammar of creation, wherein lies the story's sense of hope. Acknowledgment *is* a conscious act of creation that marks an origin, a beginning, an opening in space-time where people can feel at home as they dwell, deliberate, and know together. Emotion and discourse play a fundamental role in the creation and maintenance of this moral place of being-with-and-forothers, a place where the giving and receiving of a caring word and heart-felt caress can grant a sense of hope to all concerned. With the workings of acknowledgment at hand it is incorrect to say, contrary to Steiner's contention, that "We have no more beginnings." In fact, as I hope to show, these workings are so much a part of the ontological structure of human existence that no "grammar of nihilism"—be it of the scientific or deconstructive kind—can deny their life-giving capacity. On the contrary, the doing of "good" science and "good" deconstruction presupposes the presence and vitality of acknowledgment.

In differing with Steiner on these matters, I will have occasion, as he does, to introduce Western religion into the unfolding story of acknowledgment. For this specific phenomenon, being what it is and doing what it does, necessarily brings to mind a central question of religion regarding what it means to be a "beginning" arising from a creative act. How is acknowledgment possible? How can it be that human beings are capable of opening themselves to others, of responding "Here I am" to a call for help ("Where art thou?")? My phenomenological treatment of these questions will require that I, as much as possible, keep my nose to the empirical grindstone. In so doing, I will discuss how the ontological structure of existence that makes possible acknowledgment—*and thus its use by any institutionalized religion*—is also an originating force for the human propensity to wonder about "who we really are" and "where we really came from." Scientists who are interested in the occurrence of the Big Bang and related phenomena (e.g., singularities, black holes) take us a *long* way in answering these questions, for they are trained to be expert acknowledgers, and if they have a tolerance for the metaphysical, they may even end up contributing to the grammar and rhetoric of what has come to be called "theistic science" or the theory of "intelligent design." Steiner omits any discussion of this field of study, which contests the bifurcation between science and religion that one finds in his work. A phenomenological assessment of acknowledgment, however, encourages one not only to take an interest in this field but also *to try to keep the conversation going* between science and religion—even when their respective advocates have had enough and are fed up with their interlocutors' ways of thinking. Remember, the story of acknowledgment speaks of creation and hope.

From *The Life-Giving Gift of Acknowledgment.* Reproduced with permission of Purdue University Press.

Endnotes

1. Ernest Becker, *The Denial of Death* (New York: The Free Press, 1973), 152–153.

2. This is not to suggest, of course, that all negative acknowledgment is harmful. For example, being shown by a student in a caring way that I have done something "wrong" in class can be beneficial to all concerned.

3. *As* Calvin O. Schrag notes, "the blurring of the grammar of acknowledgment with the grammar of recognition is one of the most glaring misdirections of modern epistemology." See his *God as Otherwise than Being: Toward a Semantics of the Gift* (Evanston, Ill.: Northwestern University Press, 2002), 117–118.

4. Considering the definition of "recognition" found in the *Oxford English Dictionary* (OED)—"The action or fact of perceiving that some thing, person, etc., is the same as one previously known; the mental process of identifying what has been known before; the fact of being thus known or identified"—can also help to distinguish this phenomenon from acknowledgment as I have just defined it. The phenomenon of acknowledgment entails more than the mental process of identifying what has been known before. Thanks is owed to Lisbeth Lipari for this insight. In his *The Struggle of Recognition: The Moral Grammar of Social Conflicts,* trans. Joel Anderson (Cambridge, Mass.: MIT Press, 1996), Axel Honneth offers a comparative analysis of the role of recognition in the philosophies and social theories of G. W. F. Hegel and George Herbert Mead. He also makes mention of the work of Immanuel Kant, Karl Marx, Georges Sorel, and Jean-Paul Sartre. From my perspective, what Honneth has to say about these individuals' respective assessments of "recognition " *(Anerkennung:* to ascribe to individuals "some *positive* status") would be more accurately expressed with the term "acknowledgment" (cf. "Translator's Note," viii–ix). Throughout the book, Honneth's discussion of his central topic remains on an abstract philosophical level. No case studies are presented to clarify the practical application of his assessments. This omission, too, adds to the confusion of how acknowledgment and recognition differ in scope and function. A host of case studies are presented throughout the present work as a way of avoiding this problem. A systematic study of acknowledgment requires that one integrate theory and practice as carefully as possible.

5. Stanley Cavell, *The Claim of Reason: Wittgenstein, Skepticism, Morality, and Tragedy* (New York: Oxford University Press, 1979), 389, 435.

6. Stanley Cavell, *Must We Mean What We Say?* (New York: Cambridge University Press, 1976), 255.

7. Ludwig Wittgenstein, *On Certainty,* ed. G. E. M. Anscombe and G. H. von Wright, trans. Denis Paul and G. E. M. Anscombe (New York: Harper and Row, 1969), #378.

8. In all fairness to Cavell, I suspect that he might contend that his assessment of acknowledgment in light of his readings of such Shakespearean plays as *King Lear* (in *Must We Mean What We Say?* 267–354), as well as *Antony and Cleopatra, As You Like It, Hamlet, Othello,* and others (in *The Claim of Reason,* 329–496), does have something to say about the life-giving capacity of acknowledgment. I would not disagree. Indeed, the genius of

Shakespeare is far-reaching and Cavell's painstaking reading of the Bard is, to say the least, quite fine. Still, as I hope to make clear, the life-giving capacity of acknowledgment is considerably more complex and extensive than Cavell admits.

9. Brant R. Burleson and Erina L. MacGeorge, "Supportive Communication," in *Handbook of Interpersonal Communication,* ed. Mark L. Knapp and John A. Daly (Thousand Oaks, Calif.: Sage, 2002), 374–424.

10. My use of the term "evolution" here reflects my appropriation of various arguments set forth in the literature of evolutionary psychology. See, for example, Robert Wright, *The Moral Animal: Evolutionary Psychology and Everyday Life* (New York: Vintage Books, 1994), esp. 327–344.

11. Kenneth Burke, *Permanence and Change,* 2nd rev. ed. (New York: Bobbs-Merrill, 1954), 37.

12. Plato, *Gorgias,* trans. W. D. Woodhead, in *The Collected Dialogues of Plato,* ed. Edith Hamilton and Huntington Cairns (Princeton, N.J.: Princeton University Press, 1961), 456b–c. For a discussion that takes exception to Plato's unflattering representation of Gorgias, see Bruce McComiskey, *Gorgias and the New Sophistic Rhetoric* (Carbondale: Southern Illinois University Press, 2002).

13. See Garry Wills, *Lincoln at Gettysburg: The Words That Remade America* (New York: Simon & Schuster, 1992).

14. Richard M. Weaver, *The Ethics of Rhetoric* (Chicago: Henry Regnery, 1965), 175, 178.

15. Ibid., 175; also see Richard M. Weaver, *Visions of Order: The Cultural Crisis of Our Time* (Baton Rouge: Louisiana State University Press, 1964), 7. Praising Lincoln in this way can be called into question by certain "racist" claims that he made during his famous debates with Stephen A. Douglas during the summer and fall of 1858. I deal with this matter in greater detail in chapter nine when analyzing the present day controversy regarding the flying of the Confederate Battle Flag over the Statehouse dome in South Carolina

16. George Steiner, *Grammars of Creation* (New Haven, Conn.: Yale University Press, 2001), 9–11. Hereafter cited in the text as *GC. As* is the case with a host of books that have been published in various fields over the last fifty years and that reflect disillusion with where "progress" has taken us in the twentieth century, Steiner's contention here serves as a major warrant for the writing of his book which, as will be discussed shortly in the text, offers itself as a remedy for the condition he bemoans. This remedy, especially as it involves developing a reappreciation of theological and literary matters, also has much precedent in literatures pertaining to these fields. Commenting on what he sees to be the uniqueness of his book, Steiner notes that his book is "an *in memoriam* for lost futures and a stab at understanding their transmutation into something 'rich and strange' (though the 'richness' is, perhaps, in doubt). In another sense, I want to consider the word and concept 'creation' at a moment when Western culture and argument are so fascinated by origins" (15–16).

17. Steiner, in my humble estimation, offers a "too quick" assessment of science and deconstruction. Although I, too, at times will be critical of these enterprises, I also will have more positive things to say about them throughout the book.

18. This discussion will draw heavily from the writings of both Heidegger and Levinas. Although Steiner turns to Heidegger throughout his book as a way of emphasizing the importance of creativity in the arts and in philosophy, he avoids any specific assessment of Heidegger's understanding of acknowledgment and the role it plays in his philosophy. Chapters 2 and 3 of the present book deal with this matter in great detail. Levinas is briefly mentioned by Steiner, who credits the French philosopher with offering a "noble doctrine" of "altruism" that, in the end, fails to go "to the heart of the question": "Is there in creation an enormity of irrelevance so far as human life is concerned?" (40). With Levinas, too, however, Steiner avoids the topic of acknowledgment, which, as will be indicated in chapter 6, plays a crucial role in Levinas's theory of "the caress." In this theory, the Judaic appreciation of "acknowledgment" as a "primordial" communicative act and response ("Where art thou?" "Here I am!") receives much attention. Hence, it is interesting to note that although Steiner draws from his Judaic heritage to support his thesis about creation, he has nothing explicit to say about how acknowledgment figures in to this central question/ answer narrative structure of the Old Testament. I attend to this matter throughout the chapters of this book.

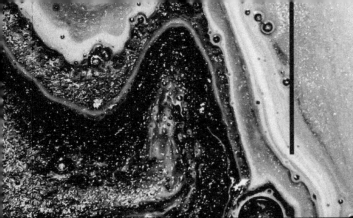

4

Organizational and Small Group Communication Ethics

What would be your dream job and work environment? Some of us dream of working within a huge organization that has a view of a city skyline; others want to work alone in a forest. To focus ourselves on the vast potential/variations within an organization, let's play a game of *Would You Rather.* Answer which choice you'd make over the alternative for the following scenarios:

Would you rather work for an organization . . .

. . .where you enjoy working with your colleagues—OR—where you don't enjoy working with your colleagues, but you get paid a little more?

. . .that has very strict policies about personal social media accounts in regards to references about the organization—OR—one that carefully monitors your work email content?

. . .that tries to lessen its environmental footprint every year—OR—one that allows you to use the copy machine as much as you want?

. . .that advances employees from within the company to reward commitment to the company—OR—often hires new employees for a fresh perspective?

. . .that allows employees to volunteer in the community on company time for 3 hours a month—OR—pays employees bonuses for not taking sick days?

. . .that fires the CEO for sexual harassment—OR—asks the CEO to retire to keep company stock prices steady?

These scenarios give a glimpse into the complex systems of organizations and their communication. If you think about a university club or team of which you are a member, think about how the university impacts the decisions, choices, budget, perceptions, and interactions of that club/team. Now take it

© LightField Studios/Shutterstock.com

one step further and think about how those messages, oral and written, are relayed to and within the club. This, in a nutshell, is organizational communication. This type of communication extends to both external messages as well as those internal to the organization. For example, external communication is used to communicate with the local community, constituents, stakeholders, and the general public with the use of mass media/social media and public speaking. Internal communication is used within the organization to connect with a diverse group of employees via training, hiring and firing practices, leadership, performance appraisals, advancements, policies and procedures, information dissemination, and list could continue forever but, you get the point. Organizational communication is complex, messy, and impacts us in every aspect of our lives.

In turn, organizational communication ethics is just as complex, messy, and impactful. What makes ethics within organizational communication unique is that ethical decisions are rarely made by one person but, rather, include groups of people in the process. Organizational communication ethics is also distinctive in that it covers every medium of communication from mass media, intercultural, public speaking, small group, and dyadic communication. Can you imagine how many ethical decisions and scenarios can take place within each context and amongst the varying forms of communication? There would be too many to count!

W. C. Redding's Typology of Unethical Messages (1996) helps to narrow our focus by providing us with six overarching unethical communication acts within organizations: (1) coercive, abuse of power or authority; (2) destructive, behavior that attacks a receiver; (3) deceptive, behavior that is intentionally false; (4) intrusive, monitoring behavior; (5) secretive, purposefully not disclosing information; and (6) manipulative–exploitative (Buzzanelle & Stohl, 1999). These behaviors are at the root of most unethical organizational decisions and behaviors.

To address issues such as these, using an ethical perspective lens helps to better understand the range of issues we face inside organizations. Four communication ethics perspectives are particularly relevant to organizational communication: duty ethics (code of ethics), consequentialist ethics (utilitarian), feminist ethics, and dialogic ethics. You can refer back to chapter 2 of this book for a general discussion of these perspectives, but what follows is how they apply specifically to organizational communication.

Duty Ethics

Often within professions and/or organizations, there are codes of ethics by which each profession is expected to behave. These codes let professionals know what the right thing to do is—what *duty* they have to uphold. The outcome of the ethical choice is not important. The choice focuses on the means, what that person has to do, that is important. For example, the Society of Professional Journalists (SPJ) has a code of ethics that clearly outlines multiple areas of expected behaviors for journalists. Within this code, there are clear guidelines as to when a journalist should keep a source's identity confidential. So, if a journalist is trying to decide whether or not the source should be revealed, the code provides the journalist a sense of duty to protect a source from harm that will guide their decision. While the SPJ Code of Ethics is too lengthy to discuss in entirety here, you may find the full code at https://www.spj.org/ethicscode.asp. In addition, organizations often use duty ethics in their training of new employees to set expectations of how employees should behave when working. Duty ethics discussions will often tie expectations to the organization's mission. This training, when reinforced through policies/procedures and day-to-day interactions, helps shape the organizational culture.

Consequentialist Ethics

The consequentialist ethical perspective is prevalent within organizational communication. This approach asks us to do that which can bring the most happiness (or least harm) for the most people involved with or impacted by the organization. Remember that the people can include employees, stakeholders, shareholders, and the public. This ethical perspective could be seen when small businesses closed their doors during the COVID-19 pandemic, even after they were told they could open, so that their employees would remain safe and healthy. Those that could do so even paid for their employees' health insurance during that time of unemployment. We also saw unethical behaviors from organizations during the COVID-19 pandemic when some companies bought sought-after toilet paper that was in short supply, and then sold it at a large increase. When looking through the consequentialist ethical lens, the focus often turns to fairness or justice for the most people. While that's admirable, it's also important to examine if under-represented people or those in the minority of any particular decision are being unjustly treated.

Feminist Ethics

According to CNBC (Connley, 2019), there were only 33 female CEOs in the top-ranked Fortune 500 companies in 2019. This is despite the fact that the general population is 53% women. The feminist ethical perspective gives a critical eye to the treatment of women and other people who are not part of the majority in power. Feminist perspectives may provide insight to ethical decisions via alternative explanations. For example, ethical decisions that support an ethic of care rather than an ethic of justice can be applied to a hypothetical situation where an employee is discovered stealing soup out of the organization's kitchen supplies. According to Carol Gilligan (1982), the ethic of justice perspective would suggest that the person must be fired just as the organization's employee handbook states. However, the ethic of care, would look further into the situation to learn the reasons for the theft. The organization might discover that the employee was desperate to take care of a large family that was going hungry due to lack of food in the home. Knowing that, the organization might not resort to firing the employee, but instead helping the employee by identifying available company and community resources to address the family's food insecurity.

Dialogic Ethics

Dialogic ethics is another ethical perspective that is especially pertinent to the building block of organizations, small group communication. Think about how organizations are structured. Usually within an organization there are departments, action groups, or virtual teams that collaborate to create a product that is better than what could be created by a single individual. Miller (2008) defines small group communication as "the social collectives, embedded in a larger environment, in which activities are coordinated to achieve individual and collective goals" (p. 1). Of course, small groups can also be the hub of discontent and failure. There are a number of issues that the small group ethicist would look at within the organization, but none more researched than the concept of *groupthink*. Groupthink (Janis, 1971) is a breakdown in the decision-making process within a highly cohesive small group when members think they are too good to make a mistake or they don't think they can express opposing views. Two of the most cited disasters of groupthink are the Bay of Pigs invasion of 1961, a failed CIA operation to oust Fidel Castro from power in Cuba and the U.S. Space Shuttle Challenger explosion of 1986 that killed seven crew members and forever changed NASA's space program (Sims, 1992). To mitigate the groupthink that can end in disaster, organizations will often set up a whistle-blowing policy or protections to offer employees safety to express concerns about problematic decisions or unethical behaviors.

By communicating in ways that exemplify the features of dialogic ethics, small groups can better their interactions between people and build relationships that foster stronger organizations. As Susan Scott (2017) states,

> Our work, our relationships, and our lives succeed or fail one conversation at a time. While no single conversation is guaranteed to transform a company, a relationship, or a life, any single conversation can. The conversation is the relationship (Foreword, x).

According to Arnett et al., (2018) dialogic ethics facilitates positive communication in its "manner of listening, attentiveness, and negotiation" (p. 205). This communication supports Buber's I/Thou philosophy of interacting with a human being as a whole person—and not as an it or, in other words, an object (Birnbaum, 1998). Communicating this way allows relationships to be real, steeped in present realities, and humanizing to all the people interacting. Wouldn't it be wonderful if all small groups interacted like this?

Chapter Activities

Our hope is that the activities in this chapter will allow you to gain personal insights to the pervasiveness of ethics throughout an organization. Although the perspectives provided are not exhaustive, they will help you consider different ways of responding and thinking that, in turn, may shift your understanding of the various communication events you might encounter in organizations. With these chapter activities, you will analyze a broad organizational perspective, specific organizational scenarios, and the building blocks of organizations by considering small group communication and leadership.

Finding Your Fit: A Website Analysis Activity

The first two activities in this chapter ask you to look at the corporate culture of organizations. In *Finding Your Fit: A Website Analysis Activity*, you will investigate organizational websites to see what they espouse to be—their public image. You'll ask yourself, "What are their values and mission? How do those align with what I know of the company and to my own values? Would I want to work there?"

Hot Topics

The next chapter activity, *Hot Topics*, continues that big picture approach and highlights companies whose missions have been tainted with illegal and unethical practices. Unfortunately, there are many current headlines that point out how organizations go down destructive paths involving poor ethical judgements. This activity allows you to learn from their mistakes.

Instructional Simulations for Ethical Dilemmas

The next few chapter activities allow you to apply your ethical reasoning to specific organizational scenarios. This chapter activity facilitates discussion about the competing values and differing needs that often swirl around ethical dilemmas. Using a simulation that addresses several stake-holders' perspectives, the "messiness" of various perceptions within ethical issues are addressed. Learning to perceive issues through multiple perspectives is paramount to your success as a student and professional.

What Choice Would You Make?

This chapter activity continues to challenge your ability to reason ethically. *What Choice Would You Make?* asks you to analyze a television episode involving professional ethics wherein, no matter what decision you make, there is no real winner. It asks you to think about, not only what you'd do, but how you'd decide and act upon this ethical dilemma.

Racism and Stereotyping in the Workplace

With the use of a real-life case study, this chapter activity prompts you to consider your responses to racist and stereotypical comments made within an organization. It puts you in a scenario that asks you to decide if, when, and how you'd act in this situation. It's a situation that is important to think through prior to being in the situation. So, really try to put yourself in this person's shoes!

Small Group Communication Ethics

The last two activities focus on small group communication. Many ethical decisions are made by small groups and the people who lead them. The *Small Group Communication Ethics* activity uses a role-playing simulation to point out the pervasive nature of communication ethics within key components of small groups. You and your classmates will have fun enacting various roles!

Building the Character to Lead

This chapter activity will ask you to reflect on your leadership within small groups and to tap into the tension between fear and courage. You will ask yourself, "What fears are limiting my ability to ethically lead?" Powerful insights about yourself can result from this activity!

Overall, whether you are learning from the broad scope of organizational websites or from ethical self-reflection, we know you will grow in your understanding of organizations and small group communication from this chapter's activities. As you engage in them, we ask that you think about and even challenge your own perceptions. Then, most importantly, reflect on the applicability of what you are learning. In doing so, you will learn to be mindful of the ethical dimensions of organizations and small groups.

References

Arnett, R. C., Fritz, J. M. H., & Bell McManus, L. M. (2018). *Communication ethics literacy: Dialogue and difference* (2nd ed.). Kendall Hunt.

Birnbaum, R. (1998). The uniqueness of Martin Buber. *Modern Age, 40*(4), 389.

Buzzanell, P. M. & Stohl, C. (1999). The Redding tradition of organizational communication scholarship: W. Charles Redding and his legacy, *Communication Studies, 50*: 4, 324–336, DOI: 10.1080/10510979909388503

Connley, C. (2019). The number of women running Fortune 500 companies is at a record high. *CNBC Make It*. https://www.cnbc.com/2019/05/16/the-number-of-women-running-fortune-500-companies-is-at-a-record-high.html

Gilligan, C. (1982). *In a different voice: Psychological theory and women's development*. Harvard University Press.

Janis, I. L. (1971). Groupthink. *Psychology Today*, 5, 43–46, 74–76.

Miller, K. I. (2008). Organizational communication. In The International Encyclopedia of Communication, W. Donsbach (Ed.). Online publication. http://doi.org/10.1002/9781405186407.wbieco018

Redding, W. C. (1996). Ethics and the study of organizational communication: When will we wake up? In J. A. Jaksa & M. S. Pritchard (Eds.), *Responsible communication: Ethical issues in business, industry, and the professions* (pp. 17–40). Hampton Press.

Scott, S. (2017). *Fierce conversations: Achieving success & in life, one conversation at a time*. Penguin Random House.

Sims, R. R. (1992). Linking groupthink to unethical behavior in organizations. *Journal of Business Ethics, 11*(9), 651–662.

Finding Your Fit

A Website Analysis Activity

Have you ever joined a student organization, held an internship, or participated on a team and thought, I belong here! If so, you have had a glimpse of a *dwelling place*. The term dwelling place is used to describe an organization's uniqueness created by specific practices they establish and stories they share. For instance, Zappos, an online retailer in Nevada, has weekly parades through the offices of their headquarters. Zappos' parades are led by different departments and reflect their unconventional culture. Stories of Zappos' generous customer service include welcoming returns, spending hours talking with customers, and even sometimes sending a pizza to a hungry caller (Ferrell et al., 2015). Likewise, universities, colleges, nonprofit organizations, and businesses have their own particular traditions, customs, and practices, all of which contribute to their uniqueness and make them different from other organizations.

In this activity, you will explore the concept of *dwelling place* by choosing an organization and evaluating if it is a fit for you professionally. In your evaluation, consider the organization's communication practices, values, and ethical perspective(s) as reflected in their mission statement, code of conduct, and other essential documents posted on their website.

Based on the organization you select for this activity, you will increase your *knowledge* by analyzing:

- What are the core communication practices and values in the organization's mission statement?

- How are the core communication practices and values reflected in the organization's code of conduct?

© G-Stock Studio/Shutterstock.com

In this activity, you will learn *skills* by investigating:

- What ethical perspective(s) are reflected in an organization's mission statement?
- What ethical perspective(s) are evident in other essential documents and videos on the organization's website?

In this activity, you will reflect on your own *values* by inquiring:

- What ethical values are important to you in the workplace?
- In what ways are your values reflected in the organization's communication?

In this activity, you will take *action* by evaluating:

- How could an organization's communication practices and ethical values provide a potential fit professionally or a *dwelling place* for you?
- How could you contribute your knowledge and communication skills to this organization?

The Activity

Part I: Preparation and Research

1. Select an organization, read the organization's mission statement, vision statement, and employee code of conduct.

2. Listen to the organization's supporting videos to identify their communication practices and ethical values.

3. After completing your initial research, respond to the following questions based on the organization's website.

    a) What are the organization's core communication practices and values? b) What particular good is this organization protecting and promoting? c) How does it appear to provide a *dwelling place* for its employees, customers, and/or community?

    _____

    _____

    _____

    _____

    _____

    _____

4. What ethical perspective(s) is reflected in the organization's communication? How so?

    _____

    _____

    _____

5. Given your findings, how could this organization be a potential *dwelling place* for you professionally? Consider your response in light of your own values.

---

6. Summarize your findings to share with the class.

Part II: Class Discussion

1. Based on the organization you chose, what communicative practices are embedded in their organizational culture?

2. What ethical values do you share with the organization you researched? How do your ethical values differ from the organization?

3. What ethical perspective(s) are reflected in the organization's communication?

4. How does identifying the ethical perspective(s) contribute to your understanding of the organization being (or not being) a potential *dwelling place*?

References

Arnett, R. C., Fritz, J. M. H., & Bell McManus, L. M. (2018). *Communication ethics literacy: Dialogue and difference* (2nd ed.). Kendall Hunt.

Ferrell, O. C., Fraedrich, J., & Ferrell, L. (2015). *Business ethics: Ethical decision making and cases.* Cengage Learning.

Levinas, E. (1969). *Totality and infinity: An essay on exteriority.* (A. Lingis, Trans.). Duquesne University Press.

Hot Topics

If you turn on the evening news or look at any news feed, you will see many organizations that find themselves in controversial situations that resulted in negative publicity. This activity will bring to light ethical controversies that occur in all sectors of the marketplace.

Many organizations have some type of mission, vision, or values statement designed to communicate succinctly the organizational culture. These statements act as guidelines to hold the organization and the employees accountable for their actions. But what happens when organizations stray away from their mission, vision, and values? Who holds these companies accountable for their actions? Have you ever not bought a product or not shopped at a store because you felt the company's values did not align with your values? This activity will allow you and your classmates to examine various industries to find Hot Topics that have ethical implications for society.

In this activity, you'll increase your *knowledge* by thinking about and asking:

- What organizations have strayed from their mission, vision, and values statement?

- What do you know about these organizations?

You'll have the opportunity to learn *skills* by considering:

- How can you engage in being a resourceful consumer?

- What decisions do you make, and why, with your purchasing power?

You can consider your own *values* and that of others by asking:

- What makes an organization worthy of your business?

- What values are important for you as a consumer?

Putting what you learn into *action* means considering:

- How does an organization's mission, vision, and values statement influence your decision-making?

- How can you protect and promote various organizations' ethical standards?

- What is required of you to be a resourceful consumer?

The Activity

You and a partner will be assigned an industry. Within that industry, you will need to find an example of a controversial situation that became a hot topic for a specific organization (e.g., EpiPen's sudden price increase, Toyota's brake scandal, Wells Fargo's banking scandal, Volkswagen's emission test, college admissions cheating). You will then research the hot topic that has ethical implications for everyone involved.

You and your partner will lead the class in a 12 to 15 minute discussion about the topic by introducing the controversy, presenting the organization's mission, vision, and values statement, and offering who you believe is accountable for the controversy. Prepare three open-ended questions that will promote discussion. The first question should be about the organization and the hot topic. The second question should focus on what is considered the good in this particular case. The last question should ask about the ethical implications.

Additional Resources

Arnett, R., Fritz, J. M. H., & Bell McManus, L. M. (2018). Communication ethics literacy: Dialogue and difference (2nd ed.). Kendall Hunt.

MacIntyre, A. (2007). After virtue (3rd ed.). University of Notre Dame Press.

Stebbins, S., Comen, E., Sauter, M. B. & Stockdale, C. (2018, February). Bad reputations: America's top 20 most-hated companies Retrieved from https://www.usatoday.com/story/money/business/2Leeanne018/02/01/bad-reputation-americas-top-20-most-hated-companies/1058718001/

Instructional Simulations for Ethical Dilemmas

When you are working on a group project for a class or student organization, how do you address ethical challenges that arise? How would you respond to a group member who misses mandatory meetings to care for a family member and then relies on you to do the majority of the work? What is your response to group members who want to cut corners on a service-learning project?

With the trend toward more team-based projects and greater collaboration in the workplace, you will be expected to be an effective team leader and member. Instructional simulations or group role-plays allow you to practice identifying ethical dilemmas and applying ethical perspectives to learn more about ethics and communication.

In this activity, you will increase your *knowledge* by analyzing:

- What ethical dilemmas are present in the instructional simulation?

- What ethical perspective(s) best respond(s) to the ethical dilemma (e.g., virtue ethics, dialogic ethics, consequentialist ethics, etc.)?

In this activity, you will have the opportunity to learn *skills* by investigating:

- How will I apply an ethical perspective to the ethical dilemma?

- What speaking skills are needed to communicate about ethical dilemmas?

- What is the role of ethical listening?

In this activity, you can consider your own *values* by inquiring:

- What ethical values motivate me in the workplace?

- What values are important to me in communicating with my peers, co-workers, leaders, and other stakeholders in the workplace?

In this activity, you can put what you learn into *action* by evaluating:

- What actions should be taken in the short term, mid-range, and long term to address the ethical dilemmas in the simulation?

- How does the ethical perspective you applied influence your communication choices, attitudes, and listening?

The Activity

In this activity, you will analyze a situation for ethical dilemmas and explore possible responses based on ethical perspectives. As you work with your classmates, you will also hone your leadership abilities and develop your group communication skills. Based on the instructional simulation and participant role assigned, consider how you will role-play your part in the simulation and select an ethical perspective that best responds to the situation.

1. Each small group should review the background for one of the simulations *before* your discussion at https://danielsethics.mgt.unm.edu/teaching-resources/simulations.asp. If your professor has assigned a specific simulation for you to examine, read that one. If you are encouraged to choose your own, do so in cooperation with your group.

2. Divide your group so that each person has a role in the simulation and read the related information for that role. Some roles can be shared if your simulation does not have a different role for each person in your group.

3. From the vantage point of your selected role, prepare for your group discussion by considering at least one ethical dilemma in the situation and the action you think you should take in the short term, mid-range, and long term to address it.

4. Choose an ethical perspective to guide your communication during the role-play.

5. Once everyone is prepared for the role assigned, your group will discuss the specifics of the situation and consider the desired outcomes. The discussion or role-play will last approximately 45 minutes.

Discussion Questions

1. What did you see as the ethical dilemma(s)?

2. What ethical perspective did you apply and how did this ethical perspective influence your communication with others in your group?

3. What action did you determine should be taken in the short term, mid-range, and long term?

Sample Simulation

The *National Farm and Garden Simulation* addresses the safety, development, and manufacturing of a product as well as risk management, media, and public relations (L. Ferrell & O. C. Ferrell, n. d.). The context of the simulation is a strategy meeting of the CEO and department leaders to discuss a product defect. (For more information on the simulation, see https://danielsethics.mgt.unm.edu/pdf/National%20Farm%20and%20Garden%20Simulation.pdf). The following questions lead to a discussion of the simulation from the perspective of consequentialist ethics or utilitarianism. For philosophers Jeremy Bentham and John Stuart Mill, a utilitarian perspective claims the ethical decision leads to the maximum utility or the greatest good for the greatest number.

1. How would you apply utilitarianism to this situation?

2. Did National Farm and Garden (NFG) have a reasonable basis for reducing the time for research and development to release the Turbo Tiller and for using the shield design from the Ultra Tiller even though it would be difficult to reattach the protective shield after cleaning?

3. In response to the safety risks of the Turbo Tiller product, what actions will produce the greatest good and do the least harm? (e.g., safety training for employees and customers, recalling the product, and/or redesigning the safety shield, etc.)

4. Following your analysis, what proposal best serves all stakeholders (e.g., employees, customers, community members, etc.)? Consider this question for the short term, mid-range, and long term.

5. From a communication ethics perspective, what internal changes would you advise the leaders of NFG to make?

6. Additional Resources are available here (https://danielsethics.mgt.unm.edu/teaching-resources/simulations.asp).

Reference

Ferrell, L., & Ferrell, O. C. (n.d.). Daniels fund ethics initiative: Simulations & applications [Role-Play exercise 3: National farm and garden. Houghton Mifflin Co.]. https://danielsethics.mgt.unm.edu/pdf/National%20Farm%20and%20Garden%20Simulation.pdf

Additional Resources

Christensen, C. R. (1987). *Teaching and the case method*. Harvard Business School.

Johannesen, R. L. (2002). *Ethics in human communication* (5th ed.). Waveland Press, Inc.

Lebacqz, K. (1985). *Professional ethics: power and paradox*. Abingdon Press.

Neher, W. W., & Sandin, P. J. (2007). *Communicating ethically: Character, duties, consequences, and relationships*. Pearson Education, Inc.

Tompkins, P. (2019). *Practicing communication ethics: Development, discernment, and decision making* (2nd ed.). Routledge.

What Choice Would You Make?

Ethical Decision-Making Involving Professional Ethics, Personal Values, and Whistle Blowing

No matter what job you have, there are usually a set of standards that are expected. Some of those standards are more rigid than others, but they are there. So, whether you are working at a career, or in a part time or volunteer position, there may come a time when your professional standards are in conflict with your personal values. Often, both sides of an ethical dilemma are important and have value—that's what makes it difficult. It is called a dilemma for a reason. How you handle these types of situations can impact your professional reputation, personal integrity, and job retention. Therefore, thoughtful and informed ethical decision-making is needed for these types of situations.

This YouTube-based discussion helps to prepare you for the difficult ethical dilemmas you may face. It asks you to recognize ethical dilemmas, perceive their complexity, practice discussing the conflicting values, and practice ethical decision-making.

In this activity, you will increase your *knowledge* by analyzing:

- What are the differences between legal, professional, and personal ethics?

- How would you recognize a whistle-blower?

You'll have the opportunity to learn *skills* by considering:

- What process can you use to make ethical decisions?

- What is the best way to articulate your perspective when perceived differently by others?

© Rei Imagine/Shutterstock.com

In this activity, you will reflect on your own *values* by inquiring:

- Which of the following do you think should be the most important when making ethical decisions: lawful behavior, following the courage of your conviction, or professional ethics?

In this activity, you can put what you learn into *action* by evaluating:

- What would you do in this situation?

- How have you handled situations like this in the past?

The Activity

The discussion will be based on an episode called, *Honor Code,* from the television show *The Practice* (season 6, episode 7, available on a streaming service).

Part I: Start watching this clip at the beginning of the episode and pause it at 15:45.

Write down your answers to these reflection questions before watching more of the episode:

1. What would you do in this situation?

2. Why would you make that decision?

3. What ramifications might there be with that decision?

4. What do you think will happen next?

   a. Did you base your answer to #4 on the fact that it was a TV show, your own experience, or your own conviction as to what is right and wrong?

Part II: Complete watching the episode up to 17:43.

Answer the following questions:

1. What is your reaction to this outcome?

2. Ethical dilemmas are often a conflict between two strongly felt ethical values. What do you see as the conflict of values in this episode?

3. Who was or were the whistle-blower(s) in this episode? Jimmy? Eugene? Dr. Harold Manning, V. P. of Medical Affairs for Brentford Mutual Insurance Company?

   a. What kind of courage is necessary to be a whistle-blower?

   b. Would you be able to make that decision? Why or why not?

Discussion Questions

Your instructor may follow up with a class discussion regarding the following areas:

1. When we first paused the video and you wrote down your thoughts, who did you think was more correct: Eugene or Jimmy?

2. Whether you are Team Eugene or Team Jimmy, complete the ethical decision-making steps from each of their perspectives (Tompkins, 2019):

   a. Recognizing that there is an ethical issue

   b. What are the facts?

   c. What are the various ethical responses?

   d. Evaluate these alternatives from different points of view (including short-term and long-term consequences.)

   e. Once you've enacted your choice, you would then act and then reflect on that chosen course of action.

3. What can we learn from each of the alternative points of view?

4. Julie Belle White-Newman (1990) discusses one's ability to be "morally flabby" versus "morally fit." In other words, if we aren't practicing making highly ethical decisions in the little things in our life, when the big ethical dilemmas of life hit us, we aren't morally fit enough to make the tough, ethical decisions. With morally flabby versus fit in mind, how can we explain Jimmy's less-than-ethical previous misconduct and his decision in this episode?

   a. Did he learn from those mistakes?

   b. How can we learn from our mistakes to make us more morally fit rather than letting it define us?

References

Tavlo, T. (2018, March 6). *The Practice S06E07 Honor Code* [video]. YouTube. https://www.youtube.com/watch?v=PkZfzdIN_Kw

White-Newman, J. B. (1990). A position paper on teaching communication ethics in the 1990's: Avoiding those pitfalls that encourage naiveté/cynicism. In J. A. Jaksa (Ed.), *Proceedings from the First Annual Communication Ethical Conference* (pp. 264–278). Western Michigan University.

Additional Resources

Jenson, J. V. (1987). Ethical tension points in whistleblowing. *Journal of Business Ethics, 6*(4), 321–328. https://doi.org/10.1007/BF00382941

Tompkins, P. S. (2019). *Practicing communication ethics: Development, discernment, and decision making* (2nd ed.). Routledge.

Racism and Stereotyping in the Workplace

Imagine it's your first day of work in a new organization. More specifically, imagine it's your first day of work after 11 years in the U.S. Navy as a helicopter pilot. As a 30-something white man with a military haircut, you are starting work at a company that flies helicopters to the oil rigs in the Gulf of Mexico. Most employees commute to work and spend a week living in company-provided housing before going home for a week. The company provides housing that includes other people who are scheduled to work.[1] The first few weeks at work, you witness and experience racism and stereotyping. How do you respond?

In this activity, you will increase your *knowledge* by considering:

- What is racism? How does it affect your own life?

- What ethical perspectives are relevant to this situation? How are they defined?

In this activity, you will learn *skills* by:

- Creating a script of what you would say if you were involved in a situation where racism or stereotyping are present.

- Creating a plan to ensure that employees are treated with equity.

In this activity, you will reflect on your own *values* by:

- Examining different ethical perspectives, how they relate to racism and stereotyping, and how those perspectives reflect your own values.

- Asking questions about how racism and stereotyping affect society.

In this activity, you could take *action* by:

- Investigating how your workplace and/or university handles complaints about racist, sexist, or anti-LGBTQIA behavior.

- Working with your workplace or university to strengthen policies that create an equitable workplace.

The Activity

1. Read through the following information and three cases. Note that all of these cases are true stories that happened in the early 2000s. At the time these situations occurred, it was thought that these stories about racism wouldn't be relevant in a few years.

2. After you have read all the information, create groups of three to five people.

---

[1] These case studies were originally presented in a conference paper at the 2007 National Communication Association conference in Chicago.

3. Answer the discussion questions together.

4. After you have discussed the questions, your instructor will have you talk about the three most important takeaways from this activity.

Tale #1

The first night I checked in to the trailer [most of the pilots fly a week on and a week off and live away from home when they are working; they all stay in company-provided housing], there was a group of people watching television. One person had the remote and was flipping through the channels. He stopped at a movie with a Black gang leader. Another person in the room, a very senior pilot and member of the training department, shouted, "Jesus, isn't there anything on besides n*****s and f*****s?"

Tale #2

After being on the job for several days, I finally met the lead pilot at the base to which I was assigned. After the initial questions about where I was from, he asked me if I was married. I replied that I was, and his next question was, "Is she white?" I was surprised and answered yes, to which he said, "Good."

Tale #3

One assignment took me to a production platform off the coast of Texas. There was a crew of three people permanently assigned to monitor the rig. The three of them were in the kitchen area examining the work schedule for the year and checking which holidays they were scheduled to work. The one with the schedule said they were scheduled to work on Father's Day. Another started joking that it was a hard holiday for some people, especially the kids in the projects, for whom it was "Who's your father day."

Tale #4

During a weather day [a day no one can fly because of bad weather], a group of pilots was sitting in the office talking. One of the pilots works in Nigeria and was discussing the conditions there. He was complaining about some of the Nigerians who work as mechanics. At one point he said, "F*****g n****s! I mean, darned Nigerians." Another person in the room, the president of the pilots' union, said "Be careful with the racist talk. James (a Black mechanic) is downstairs and he can hear you." The pilot working in Nigeria replied, "It's okay. James is cool. I'll just talk to him."

The company where these situations occurred, stated on their website:

Our business integrity policy is a guideline to:

- *Promote honest and ethical conduct*

- *Maintain a workplace in which the integrity and dignity of each individual is valued*

- *Assure compliance with laws, rules, and regulations*

- *Assure the proper use of the company's assets (website information removed)*

They go on to note in their Code of Business Integrity that

> *The Company maintains a strong policy of equal employment opportunity for all members and applicants for employment. The Company hires, trains, promotes and compensates employees based upon job-related factors such as the individual's ability, work quality, attitude, competence and potential, as well as the Company operational needs, without regard for race, color, religion, sex, sexual orientation, national origin, citizenship, age, marital status or disability (website information redacted).*

They further go on to state that:

> *All employees have a right to work in an environment that is free of unlawful discrimination and harassment. Any form of discrimination or harassment, including sexually harassment, whether based on race, sex, color, religion, national origin, age, veteran status, or disability is unacceptable and will not be permitted. . . .Employees who are found to have engaged in unlawful discrimination or harassment, or to have contributed to the creation of an offensive or hostile work environment, will be subject to disciplinary action, up to and including termination of employment. . . .Please remember that we encourage you to raise any questions or concerns about these policies. If for any reason you are uncomfortable reporting those concerns to your supervisor or with the reporting requirements set out above, you may report concerns and violations confidentially, without giving your name [to a toll free number or a website that are not connected to the organization] (website information redacted).*

Discussion Questions

Discuss these questions and develop your group's three most important ideas you are taking away from these stories.

1. What is your initial reaction to these situations?

2. In what ways do you find these situations problematic (horrifying!) involving stereotyping and discrimination in an organization?

3. Have you experienced racism and discrimination like this at school or work? How do situations like this affect the organization's culture? How could encounters like these affect employee morale?

4. How do these situations exemplify racism and discrimination?

5. What ethical values come into play, if you were the pilot in the situation?

6. Imagine you're the brand-new employee who witnessed all of these situations. What do you do? What do you say? Come up with a response.

7. What short- and long-term actions would you take to respond to these situations? What skills would you need to respond effectively?

8. Imagine you are the Affirmative Action[2] officer in this organization. Lay out your plan for dealing with this once it's reported to you. At this point, you don't know how widespread the charges and examples of racism are. What's your first step? If you discover that this type of racism is widespread in your organization, what do you do? Create an action plan.

The Takeaway

The takeaway: What are three key ideas about racist and discriminatory communication in organizations your group can take away from this activity? **Make sure one of your takeaways is a script of what you would say in at least one of these situations**. Write your three ideas on your whiteboard, flipchart, or shared document. You will be asked to share your takeaways with the class publicly.

1.

2.

3.

---

[2] Mandated for those who receive federal funds, Affirmative Action is "a set of procedures designed to eliminate unlawful discrimination among applicants, remedy the results of such prior discrimination, and prevent such discrimination in the future. Applicants may be seeking admission to an educational program or looking for professional employment. In modern American jurisprudence, it typically imposes remedies against discrimination on the basis of, at the very least, race, creed, color, and national origin" (Affirmative Action, n.d., para. 1). Because most colleges receive federal financial aid, they are bound by Affirmative Action laws, as are any businesses that have contracts with the federal government.

Small Group Communication Ethics

Roles, Norms, Goals, Network

Ethical reasoning starts with your ability to recognize an ethical issue when you encounter it (Tompkins, 2019). When you're put into a small group for a class, it is easy to just do what is most expedient for your project and not give a lot of thought to the ethical choices you are making. However, the more you practice recognizing those ethical choices, the better prepared you will be to engage in ethical reasoning when issues arise—now and in the future. This activity is created for you to engage in a small group task while you enact a specified individual behavior. The follow-up discussion will help you to understand core components of small group communication and recognize ethical issues inherent to them.

In this activity, you will increase your *knowledge* by analyzing:

- How do the four small group communication concepts of goals, norms, roles, and communication networks impact a small group?

- What ethical issues might arise within each of those concepts?

- What process can I use to engage in ethical reasoning?

You'll have the opportunity to learn *skills* by considering:

- How can I recognize ethical issues when working in a small group? How will that influence my decisions?

In this activity, you will reflect on your own *values* by inquiring:

- What values do I hold that will propel me to pay attention to the ethical issues in which I engage?

- What makes my values important to who I am and my future profession?

In this activity, you can put what you learn into *action* by evaluating:

- What can you do within any of your small groups (teams, other classes, clubs) that will make a difference in how they engage in ethical reasoning?

- What can I do as an individual to help them make strong ethical choices?

The Activity

1. Your assigned small group (up to seven classmates) will engage in a competition. Each group will create a new name and corresponding logo for this course that includes every group member's perception of this class. Once completed, all students will vote for what they consider the best name and logo, and the winners will be acknowledged.

2. As part of the group work, you will randomly select an individualized behavior to perform. Using the grid provided, roll your virtual dice (https://rolladie.net/) by setting the die (that's the singular form for dice – this activity won't harm you! :-) to 7 for the left column and to 4 for the top row. Find the corresponding intersection of the dice on the graph to find your behavior to perform *throughout* your group's challenge of creating the new name and logo. The more you have fun with this – the better it will be!

3. Do not begin working on your group task until everyone has randomly selected their individualized assignment and is ready to begin working on the project. If this is an online course and you are working on this virtually, you may need to work synchronously using video your share ideas.

4. Work on your group assignment while enacting your individual assignment.

5. After completing the assignment, share your name and logo with the class for voting as directed by your instructor.

6. After the competition is complete, discuss the questions below to discover the ethical issues within your small group component.

Discussion Questions

Groups should discuss all of the questions first with each other and then share with the whole class.

1. What helped and hindered your group in completing your task?

2. How does your experience of this activity connect to each of the small group communication components of roles, norms, communication network, and goals?

   a. Goals: How important was it for your group to recognize competing individual goals and group goals? What are some other things you saw related to your goals?

   b. Norms: How did your individual behavior influence group norms and productivity?

   c. Networks: In what ways was it important to observe the communication networks' early formation within your group? Talk about how the following concepts influenced your group: gate-keeping and information overload as well as intentions vs. outcome (Your intention might be good, but the outcome might be negative).

3. Roles: Describe the importance of analyzing what roles the group is missing or has an overabundance of and adjusting your role to fit the needs of the group. Characteristics of leadership and the importance of followership can also be discussed. Using NCA's Credo for Ethical Communication (see chapter 1), what principles are most relevant to each of the small group components? Be specific.

4. Using the NCA Credo, brainstorm as a group the various ethical issues that might arise from the possible "roll the dice" scenarios you see on the grid.

5. How have any of these ethical issues played out for you in "real life"?

6. What are some important "take-aways" from this exercise?

Individual Assignment for Small Group Competition

	ROLES - 1	NORMS - 2	NETWORK - 3	GOALS - 4
1	You want to be the leader of the group. You are always the leader and will work hard to make certain everyone sees you as the leader.	You sing as you work & you like others to do so. You are also perceived as a "quirky" kind of person who does their own thing every once in a while. You know it just adds to the creativity of the group.	You make certain that everyone gets the chance to talk and everyone is understood.	You really need an A in this class. You'll do anything that it takes to get that A. If that means doing the entire project yourself, you'll do that.
2	You are what small group experts would call a "social loafer." You do not want to work on this project. So, you are not going to participate but, rather, you're going to be on your phone the whole time.	You are a busy person and need to work fast and get this task done. You don't have time to make friends with the people in your group. You just want to get the job done!	You like to get ahead in life. You have learned only to direct your attention to the person in charge. So, you only talk to the person who appears to be the leaders.	You want this logo to look really cool and the name to reflect the course well. In other words, you want the task to be done well. You know to be done well, you'll need everyone's input and to draw on each other's strengths.
3	You are a team player and like to get input from everyone so the best idea can be chosen.	You encourage those who aren't stating their opinions to do so. You think it's very important that everyone participates. So, you like to stop the group at the midway point and ask everyone to indicate how they are feeling about the process/product up to this point. You expect everyone to answer.	You direct all your comments to the person you know the best in the group. If you know no one, it is the person whose first name is closest to yours alphabetically.	You want to get the work done. You have a meeting with your advisor twenty minutes before the class ends so you need to get it done and get out of this class. However, you don't want anyone to know that you are going to leave in a few minutes because you still hope to be counted as present for today's work.
4	You are good at critiquing others' ideas. You do this with frequency.	You think that the people in your group are idiots. You perceive them to be immature and will let them know when they get on your nerves – which is often. You often roll your eyes at stupid ideas and give negative feedback to ideas that aren't yours.	You feel like you don't know English well enough to speak out loud. But, you can write English well. How can you let your group know this without looking inferior? You want them to know you're smart (you are taking college in a second language!)	You know that everyone must have the same expectation for a goal in order for the group to work toward it together. So, you will ask the group what their end-goal is for this task.

5	You are a great recorder for a group. You take a group picture at every meeting (even if it's virtual), take meeting notes, you post to a common site – you love that you can contribute in this way. You are a very detailed person.	You really want to win this competition. Your group needs to take it seriously. Since you don't know what the reward is, it could be an A for the entire semester. You've heard that this was a reward in the past. So, you want to mislead the other groups in the class by feeding them misinformation about the assignment. That will give your group an advantage.	Ask someone in the group if you can text them throughout the meeting. Throughout the meeting, make frequent, random remarks about process to that person only.	You really need an A in this class. That means that you'll pretend to listen to the others' ideas, but you'll just do the assignment yourself. That way, you know you'll get an A or only have yourself to blame if you don't get one.
6	You are good at breaking tension in the group by cracking jokes. You like to joke around with everyone in the group – especially making fun of your scatter-brained professor.	You like to socialize for at least 15 minutes at the start of the meeting so that the group members can get to know each other. This builds group cohesion and you know that, eventually, the group will work better because of it. So, you start by asking questions of each person and engaging with them on non-task dialogue.	You won't talk to anyone who is wearing another school's logo or colors. That person doesn't deserve your respect. You won't openly disrespect them, but you certainly won't talk to them.	You want to have a good name and logo but, most importantly, you want to be liked by all the members of your group.
7	You get excited about projects and interrupt people. This often means that you don't listen well but you make up for it with your wildly creative ideas.	You think that phones are a distraction when you're working on a group project. At the start of the project, you ask that everyone puts away their phone so everyone can focus on the task. When someone is on their phone when you're talking, you see it as a personal insult.	You have a history of having a stalker. You do not give out your personal phone number or email. You've learned not to trust anyone with any personal information. You certainly won't allow your picture to be taken or posted to social media.	You have a "hidden agenda" in that you want someone to become romantically interested in you by the end of this task.

References

National Communication Association (NCA). (1999). *Credo for ethical communication.* Retrieved January 22, 2020, from https://www.natcom.org/advocacy-public-engagement/public-policy/public-statements

Tompkins, P. S. (2019). *Practicing communication ethics: Development, discernment, and decision making* (2nd ed.). Routledge.

Building the Character to Lead

Managing Fear and Cultivating Courage Through Ethical Reflection

While much of the scholarly inquiry into communication ethics has focused on the interpersonal aspect of human communication, the intrapersonal practices of moral agents remain an important, if understudied, area of communication ethics. This area of inquiry is premised on the idea that the way in which we talk to ourselves, especially in the midst of an ethical dilemma, holds as much weight in our ethical decision-making as does dialoguing with others. When we reflect and deliberate regarding ethical matters, we delve into our past experiences, our values, and our fears. Existential philosophy is premised on the idea that as human beings we are in constant dialogue with our environment. Our values also feature prominently as we get to affirm them and test them through our actions. In the ethics literature courage is not an attribute with which we are born, but a disposition that is cultivated intentionally by moral agents through both intrapersonal and interpersonal communication.

As a moral virtue, courage features prominently in the communication ethics literature. In a scholarly survey published by Ronald C. Arnett (1987), he found that courage has been studied in communication ethics scholarship since 1915 consistently and in a variety of communicative contexts including our listening behaviors. In this context, courage can be manifested through our willingness to listen to others in just and open ways. Arnett believes that giving the powerless a voice takes courage and, when we listen to those who have limited power, often the best ideas emerge. Richard L. Johannessen and co-authors (2008) talk about courage in the context of Judeo-Christian or Western cultures. They note that "Good moral character usually is associated with the habitual embodiment of such virtues as courage, temperance, prudence (or practical wisdom), justice, fairness, generosity, patience, truthfulness" (p. 268).

More recently Paula Tompkins (2015) has explored the ways in which even silence can, at times, require some degree of courage. She offers the following example: "silence that allows Others to speak can be an act of courage" (p. 249). Outside of the academy, professional coaching experts have also echoed the centrality of courage to the practice of ethical leadership. For example, Eric Kaufmann, President of Sagatica, an executive leadership consultancy with leaders and teams at companies such as Verizon, SunPower, Dr. Bronner's, Alcon, and Cymer hones in on the importance of cultivating courage through reflection (monologue) in order to improve our performance as leaders. In his *Four Virtues of a Leader: Navigating the Hero's Journey through Risks to Results,* Kaufmann identifies courage as one of the four cardinal virtues among grit, trust, and focus.

In this activity, you'll increase your *knowledge* by thinking about and asking:

- What may be holding you back from being a better leader?

- What fears are shared by you and your classmates, and what patterns are recurring?

You'll have the opportunity to learn *skills* by considering:

- What strategies are available to manage your particular fears so they do not interfere with your ability to lead?

- How could you cultivate courage in ethical and effective ways to sharpen your leadership skills?

You can consider your own *values* and that of others by observing:

- How are your fears and your classmates' fears connected to specific cultural and ethical values?

- What is the nature of your fears and how are they connected to the anxieties of others?

Putting what you learn into *action* means inquiring:

- How can you reduce and confront your fears?

- How can you be mindful of those around you and what fears they are working to overcome?

- How can you empathize with others?

The Activity

This 3:07-minute YouTube video shows Eric Kaufmann (2016) discussing the nature of courage and its role in our ability to lead (https://www.youtube.com/watch?v5YerlJ52j2Do&t516s). Play the video first, then on a piece of blank paper, take 5 minutes to write in silence and answer the following question. Based on Kaufmann's description of courage as being undermined by fear, what is it that you fear about being a leader? What step could you take to address your fear? To become the leader you want to be, what ethical value(s) could you lean on?

References

Arnett, R. C. (1987). The status of communication ethics scholarship in speech communication journals from 1915-1985. *Central States Speech Journal, 38,* 44–61.

Johannessen, R. L., Valde, K. S., & Whedbee, K. E. (2008). *Ethics in human communication* (6th ed.). Waveland Press.

Kaufmann, E. (2016, June 28). Courage: Four virtues of a leader. [Video]. YouTube. https://www.youtube.com/watch?v5YerlJ52j2Do&t516s

Tompkins, P. S. (2015). Acknowledgment, justice, and communication ethics. *Review of Communication, 15,* 240–257.

Communication in Public and Community Activism

We live in unprecedented, extraordinary, challenging times.
An economic recession, a global pandemic, and rising racial tensions are among the issues that occupy news headlines as well as our daily thoughts. Naturally, you have questions and you have concerns. You might even want to take action to change the world for the better, as is the case for more and more young people.

There's reason to be hopeful! Interest in political engagement among college students is rising. This revival of student activism, reported in UCLA's national survey of freshmen, reveals that more than 22% of new college students attended a protest, march or rally in the previous year (Eagan et al., 2017). This is a promising trend because we must all be part of the public dialogue and conversations taking place around us to ensure a strong democracy that works for everyone.

Students, like you, recognize that education is the gateway to change and builds on a long tradition of people together studying, learning, and mobilizing for action together. This view of education, as a vehicle for the public good, is imbued with ethics and politics.

Ethics and Politics

If you're like many others, you may be okay with examining and expressing ethics, but just reading the word politics may make you cringe. So let's review a bit about how and why politics remains a central American tradition to which we must pay attention, and to which we need to think about in tandem with ethics.

Politics is the process by which we make decisions for how we will live together. For Aristotle, politics was the connection of the individual to the social through, and this is important, dialogue. In the 21st century, students are right to recognize that dialogue, expression in its highest ethical form, is largely absent from the political sphere.

Harvard professor and ethics center director Danielle Allen (2014) says politics builds a shared life with words, not brute force or war; it is an activity that flows from self-consciousness, involves the jockeying of power, and is aimed toward survival, freedom, and happiness. For her, the role of talk in politics is to recalibrate our relations to one another, through ethical communication, when they inevitably are in question or fall out of balance.

Peter Block (2008) similarly suggests that ethics and politics involve a series of choices we make that can lead to peaceful coexistence or suffering. When political decisions lead people to experience poverty, hunger, or violence, he reminds us that those situations are avoidable and unnecessary. To change those conditions requires the will to engage in politics and to express an ethical commitment to one another's well-being.

Other contemporary scholars and theorists likewise see ethics and politics as essential human practices of employing skills, knowledge, values and actions for how we will make decisions collectively about how to live together (Hess & McAvoy, 2015; Leftwich, 2004). Since it is unlikely we will all agree on how we want to live together, politics is inherently controversial (Journell, 2017) and can best be managed through ethical, critical conversations to consider diverse views and options.

Education provides a critical pathway toward pursuing positive social change when education unmasks pain, misery, and inequities. Education is the conduit to social change when it provides students with the ethical and political tools necessary to talk with and engage with others. Though education of all sides of an issue is important, when it comes time to making decisions or taking action, you have to assert yourself so that you can take a stand and justify your position. Having the heart, interest, and inclination to do something means you are not acting from a neutral position, but rather an engaged position. To best be able to act in concert with your values, access to education is the gateway to putting those values in conversation with knowledge, skills, and resources so that you can channel your time and interests toward work for a greater good (Jovanovic, 2014).

All of this talk about ethics, communication, and politics surely raises questions.

- What specifically can you do to make the world better?

- How will you do it?

- When is the right time to act and when is the right time to learn, listen, and assess?

- Who should you contact to join with in taking action?

- Recognizing that protests and other acts of resistance unfold in our cities, in what ways can you promote or engage with this important form of first amendment civic engagement?

These are just a few of the matters that require your thoughtful and ongoing consideration.

Community and Civic Engagement

The instructional turn toward civic education as connected to communication ethics reclaims our public spaces as free speech centers. That is, by learning about and participating with current, civic concerns, you acquire the democratic arts and skills surrounding speaking out, organizing with others, understanding essential government processes, and probing for ethical priorities necessary in our communities to resist oppression and discrimination in its many forms in favor of justice, equality, inclusion, and love.

You may understand democracy as a mode of governance and as a way to address differences in a pluralistic society. You may be hopeful about democracy even as you recognize that ours has been unable to provide some citizens a *more perfect union* as promised in our founding documents.

However, you may also express harsh words and sentiments in your assessment of politics as mentioned previously. You may not see politics as the rightful arena in which democracy is both negotiated and implemented. Instead, based on what you read in the news and see on television, you may understandably see politics as divisive, explosively partisan, and defined by arguing absent positive outcomes.

The time is right for you to understand your role in our political system depends upon freedom of speech and a deep consideration of ethics to impact what is otherwise a negative state of affairs. Attention to ethics and politics are collective responsibility-taking practices that build relationships *between* citizens (Bloch-Schulman & Jovanovic, 2010). That is, education that involves communication ethics, dialogue, understanding of politics, and steps toward activism embraces a tremendous potential to awaken and voice your ethical sensibilities (Jovanovic, 2014).

What you do with your knowledge matters, and as active citizens, your actions and public voice ripple out in ways we cannot always know but that we can be sure have impact. To work for impact that targets making the world better is a noble, ethical endeavor, and a just pursuit.

© Spoma Jovanovic

Chapter Activities

Bridging communication ethics and communication activism in our instructional methods offers a robust learning opportunity (Ballard et al., 2014). No one has to tell you that the assault on justice and constitutional violations we are witnessing in cities across the country are clear breaches of trust, undermining our foundations of democratic life. Communication scholars, among others, are vocal in the call for structural analyses, rhetorical competency, and the nurturing of activism as a commitment to democratic self-governance (Frey & Carragee, 2007).

If you don't have all the information about what is happening and what to do about it at your fingertips, it's not surprising. Many, if not most educational settings, omit lessons of how ordinary people have forwarded progressive reforms throughout history. As a result, you may have been cheated out of learning critical history and receiving classroom instruction on how to become active participants in promoting ethics and justice in our democracy (Zinn, 2015).

Communication Ethics and Activism

Have you ever wanted to write a letter to your local newspaper in support of or against a current ordinance? Or maybe you have wanted to attend a protest and hold a sign that puts your body on the line, along with other like-minded citizens? Taking direct action in this way often focuses our communication as expressions of dissent to bring attention to what we don't like or what we think is unfair. In this activity, you'll have an opportunity to meet and work alongside people who are on the front lines of social change. As you learn from them, you will be able to clarify your own values and actions in communicating your ethical position.

Participating in Municipal Politics

Thomas Jefferson, one of the architects of free public education, recognized that for democracy to be meaningful, its citizens had to be educated with requisite knowledge such as reading, writing, and arithmetic. Jefferson admittedly lived his own life full of contradictions as a slave owner and leader of a new world fighting for equality at the same time. Still, he advocated for the need in school to cultivate the ethical virtues of responsibility, courage, and reasonableness so necessary for interacting with others in a democracy in the pursuit of life, liberty, and happiness. He saw education as the ideal way to teach people their rights and duties, and their responsibilities and obligations. Taken together, this knowledge and these skills he argued would allow people to freely express themselves and make informed decisions in and with the company of others. We think you'll learn some about how people do that by attending a public meeting to observe what happens, learn about the topics discussed, and comment on the values communicated by public officials and ordinary citizens.

News Talks

As a college student, you surely want to contribute your voice to promoting the public welfare in a variety of ways. To do that, you need to have an understanding of what's happening in the news. With this activity, you'll follow the news and share what you learn with others in your class.

Voting, Elections, and Me

Maybe you want to campaign for an issue or candidate in an upcoming election? Or, surely you want to cast your vote on ballot items. To do so, you will need some knowledge about voting and voter issues. Voting is ethics in action, revealing both your own values and that of those running for office as well as what drives campaigns for new taxes or bond measures. In this activity, you'll have the opportunity to learn about your local voting processes as well as people and issues involved in an upcoming electoral race.

What Free Speech Boundaries, if any, Do We Want?

People around the world have traditionally taken to the streets to speak out against injustices. They do so as well on our college campuses. With this activity, you are encouraged to consider what limits, if any, should surround our freedom of expression? Whose rights should be protected in free speech issues? You will be able to consider how legal and ethical considerations overlap at times and diverge at other times in ongoing debates surrounding freedom and equality.

Social Movements

There are, of course, many ways to make learning relevant for the demands of today. One way is to connect current events and your understanding of them to past actions and history, which you'll discover in this activity about social movements. In doing so, you will learn about your place in the unfolding and rich story of what democratic engagement can achieve.

References

Allen, D. (2014). *Our declaration: A reading of the Declaration of Independence in defense of equality*. New York: Liveright.

Ballard, R. L., Bell McManus, L. M., Holba, A. M., Jovanovic, S., Tompkins, P. S., Charron, L. J. N., Hoffer (Vélez Ortiz), M. L., Leavitt, M. A. & Swenson-Lepper, T. (2014). Teaching communication ethics as central to the discipline. *Journal of the Association for Communication Administration, 33*(2), 2–20.

Bloch-Schulman, S. & Jovanovic, S. (2010). Who's afraid of politics? On the need to teach political engagement. *Journal of Higher Education Outreach and Engagement, 14*(1), 83–100.

Block, P. (2008). *Community: The structure of belonging*. San Francisco: Berrett-Koehler Publishers.

Eagan, M. K., Stolzenberg, E. B., Zimmerman, H. B., Aragon, M. C., Whang Sayson, H., & Rios-Aguilar, C. (2017). *The American freshman: National norms fall 2016*. Los Angeles: Higher Education Research Institute, UCLA.

Frey, L. R. & Carragee, K. M. (2007). *Teaching communication activism: Communication education for social justice*. Cresskill, NJ: Hampton Press.

Hess, D. E. & McAvoy, P. (2015). *The political classroom: Evidence and ethics in democratic education*. New York: Routledge.

Journell, W. (2017). *Teaching politics in secondary education: Engaging with contentious issues*. New York: State University of New York.

Jovanovic, S. (2014). The ethics of teaching communication activism. In L. R. Frey & D. L. Palmer (Eds.), *Teaching communication activism: Communication education for social justice* (pp. 105–138). New York, NY: Hampton Press.

Leftwich, A. (2004). *What is politics? The activity and its study*. Cambridge, UK: Polity Press.

Zinn, H. (2015). *A people's history of the United States*. New York: Harper Perennial Modern Classics.

Communication Ethics and Activism

Why and How People Protest, Demonstrate, and Resist

Some people, maybe you, believe that in order for you to be heard, you literally have to *take to the streets*. That is called protesting. Often to be heard in a democracy, we have to engage in more than just social media posts, writing our Congressional Representatives, or talking to our friends and neighbors. Sometimes we have to take to the streets in large groups in order to be heard. Doing so often requires a call to action at the grassroots level, to work for our collective well-being and to end social inequalities where they persist, striving to reclaim our deeply held human values of equality, liberty, community, and respect that a democracy requires. Government officials and processes are important to the functioning of our country, but the power of people working together is the root of democratic action and a fundamental right. As per the U.S. Constitution's First Amendment:

> *Congress shall make no law respecting an establishment of religion or prohibiting the free exercise thereof; or abridging the freedom of speech, or of the press; or the right of the people peaceably to assemble, and to petition the Government for a redress of grievances.*

Throughout history, people have launched direct actions for change to ensure equality, justice, fairness, and inclusion. For instance, it took nearly 100 years of conversations, protests, and lobbying efforts, but finally women achieved the right to vote in 1920. Carpenters in Philadelphia back in 1791 first raised the issue of the need to limit the workday to 8 hours and by 1937, that goal was signed into law. The Civil Rights Movement in the 1950s and 60s brought sweeping changes for racial equality. High school and college students were at the forefront of integrating lunch counters and then other public spaces. In 1990, people with disabilities cheered when the American Disabilities Act was signed into law to prevent unnecessary discrimination. We all observed widespread protests around the world in response to the death of George Floyd at the hands of a police officer in Minnesota throughout 2020 in pursuit of justice of Black lives. Maybe you even participated in some of these.

Activists and organizers labor to raise attention about issues generally affecting people who on their own do not hold much power. Combining voices creates greater impact over time. Activism can be a powerful, invigorating, creative experience. It is fairly common to see activists cheering, laughing, and celebrating. The work can also be frustrating without quick fixes because solutions are complex and systemic. Activists commonly feel a sense of moral outrage when the changes they see necessary are slow in coming.

In this activity, you'll increase your *knowledge* by thinking about:

- What injustices persist in your community, state, country, and world?

- Who in your community is working to confront these injustices?

You'll have the opportunity to learn *skills* by considering:

- What writing and speaking strategies and skills do activists use?

- How is activism part of the tool kit of ethical civic engagement actions?

You can consider your own *values* and that of others by asking:

- What ethical values drive activists?

- What same or different ethical values are important to you in responding to injustices?

Putting what you learn into *action* means asking:

- What kinds of messages and actions do activists rely upon to create change?

- When is protest an ethical *and* effective choice? What other forms of expression and action could they use?

- What are the pros and cons of different forms of expression and action?

The Activity

Even if you have never signed a petition, you can learn a lot about activism, and yourself, by joining with others, and/or observing activists' work.

Part I: Attend a march or protest (or other direct action such as a letter-writing drive, canvassing event, or political campaign). The key for you is to be in the presence of activists to learn what is happening, what the activists know that you do not, and reflect on the meaning and impact and activist actions. Ask questions, even if that may feel uncomfortable at first. Keep in mind that activists will be eager to talk with you. Plan on spending at least 1 hour at your event but be prepared to spend more time, depending on the action. If there are speakers, stay and listen to them. Look carefully at what else is happening around you.

Part II: Write an analysis after reading the assigned chapter for this activity and by first spending some time thinking about how the action you attended connects to your course readings, classroom discussions, and your own values. Remember, you will have met people who are passionate about correcting injustices, people who have grit and determination. Consider what ethical values and ethical perspectives drive them in their struggle for justice and how they respond to setbacks.

Tips for organizing your paper:

1. Use the introduction to feature a short story, observation, or personal reflection that highlights the main thing you learned about ethics and activism.

2. Provide details of the event/action. You may want to talk about the location and why it may have been chosen for this action. As you consider the many messages you saw and heard (on signs and from talk), see if you can distill them into a theme or two. Who was at this direct action? Young people? Old? Both? Races? Genders? If you went with a classmate, do you think that had an impact on how you acted and what you saw? How so or not?

3. Tell us about what you learned in your conversation(s) with activists. How did their values push you to think about or reconsider your own? What was inspiring or disappointing to you and why?

4. How was the protest you attended (or other direct action) part of a larger set of actions? Sum up how you see ethics and activism operating best together.

5. Explain why protest was selected as the choice of expression rather than other forms. Do you believe it was/is effective? Why or why not? What ethical values are the basis for your reasoning?

6. Include two or more meaningful references to course readings.

7. Include a photograph of you at the event.

Reference

Jovanovic, S. (2019). Communication, dialogue, and student activism. In J. L. DeVitis & Pietro A. Sasso (Eds.), *Student activism in the academy: Its struggles and promise* (pp. 21–34). Myers Education Press.

Additional Resources

Jovanovic, S., Congdon, M., Miller, C., & Richardson, G. (2015). Rooting the study of communication activism in an attempted book ban. *Partnerships: A Journal of Service-Learning and Civic Engagement, 6*(1), 115–135.

Jovanovic, S., & Russell, V. (2014). Voices of grassroots activists: Dollars and sense in the city. *Carolinas Communication Annual, 30,* 19–33.

Participating in Municipal Politics

To see democracy in action, you do not have to look far. Everything from parking rules to water quality and park amenities emerges from local decision-making. But, if you don't know how to best interact with the mayor or other government officials, you may be like a lot of other people who simply throw their hands up and say, there's nothing we can do. Well, democracy is not called rule by the leaders. Democracy is literally, rule by the people. To fulfill obligations as citizens or residents, we need to know how to participate in local or municipal politics. Indeed, local politics often have more influence on our lives than national politics and elections do, even though national politics and elections get more media coverage.

When we talk about municipal politics, we're referring to the most local political action that takes place in municipalities such as cities, counties, towns, special districts, and school districts. For most of us, our greatest opportunity to meet elected representatives, staff members, and appointed officials is at the local level. There, we may relay our own experiences and stories in hopes of effecting change (Britt & Alexander, 2019). We also have greater chances of effecting change at the local and municipal levels.

How and where you decide to participate in democracy will likely depend on the range of options with which you are familiar. For instance, most of us know that by the time we reach 18 years of age, we will have the right to vote. That's a basic, foundational way to use your voice and engage in civic matters.

There are so many more ways, however, to influence local matters. People who are active in municipal politics work together to make sure the right stakeholders and decision makers meet. They understand that good decision-making depends on good participatory processes (Carlee, 2019). You can jumpstart your learning curve in discovering how municipal politics works by putting yourself in the middle of some of the action, watching what others say and do, asking questions, and investigating the many options for you to engage with others in the public sphere (Nabatchi & Leighninger, 2015).

© Spoma Jovanovic

With this assignment, you'll increase your *knowledge* by considering:

- How and where do local meetings take place and what opportunities exist for resident involvement there?

- What resources exist that you can research to help you better understand controversial local issues?

- How are local issues and political processes similar to or different from national issues and processes?

You'll have the opportunity to learn *skills* by considering:

- What is required of you to construct fieldnotes with facts and impressions as a form of ethnographic research?

- How can you use your communication skills and knowledge to participate in local and municipal politics and decision-making?

You can consider your own *values* and that of others by asking:

- In what ways do elected and appointed leaders express respect (or not) toward residents seeking to be engaged in municipal politics?

- What issues at the local level am I most drawn to and why? What does that say about my own values and preferences about my local community?

- As you review your fieldnotes, what did you focus on and how did that reveal what ethical values you brought into the observation?

Putting what you learn into *action* means asking:

- What formal and informal routes exist for citizens to express themselves?

- How are different views invited into (or not) civil discourse?

The Activity

Attend a public meeting. Doing so is a simple, accessible way to see your elected officials and staff members at work, as well as to see how citizens interact with them. For this assignment, consider going to a meeting of your city council, county commissioners, or board of education, for instance. These meetings are open to the public, often have time for public comments on any subject, and operate by formal procedures for addressing agenda items, typically following Robert's Rules of Order. Plan on staying for 1–1/2 to 2 hours. Look at your local government (city, county, school board, planning, and zoning, etc.) websites to determine days and times of upcoming meetings.

Once you arrive at the meeting location, make sure you've allowed ample time to find parking and be prepared to pass through security checks, if required. You may need to turn off your phone and other devices and leave food and drink behind.

Find a seat and begin taking detailed notes on the content and the talk/conversation(s) that arise in the meeting. These fieldnotes are a form of research used by ethnographers who study different cultures, groups, and organizations to understand how they operate, their rules of interaction, and the values that permeate their talk (Goodall, 2000). You will use your fieldnotes to help you write the paper to complete the assignment. Don't worry if you don't understand everything that is being discussed, for instance, zoning or achievement tests or wastewater treatment. Keep taking notes and then later, you will do an additional archival search to learn more about what you were introduced to at the meeting. If you are nervous about attending a public meeting, it may help you feel more comfortable by watching a prior meeting online, if they are recorded and digitally archived in your municipality.

As you observe the meeting, consider how local government officials involve or dismiss residents that are speakers from the floor. Look at officials speaking and not speaking. How do they invite and respond to questions from the audience? How well do they listen to stories presented and how do you know? You may also want to consider how residents interact with their local officials. Are they deferential to political power? How can you tell? Are they disruptive and if so, in what ways? How did they construct their stories or facts to provide a compelling presentation?

Reflection Instructions

1. First, recap the main ideas presented at the meeting.

2. Second, go deeper into discussion about one topic. To do this, include additional research (archival search) about a concept you heard about at the meeting but were not entirely familiar to gain additional knowledge about the history, controversies, and regulations surrounding the local matter you heard discussed. Include this research (and cite it) by integrating it with what was discussed at the meeting.

3. Third, connect what you learned from the meeting and additional research with one or more ethical perspectives to clarify what values you observed.

References

Britt, L. L., & Alexander, R. (2019). Stories communities tell: How deliberative practitioners can work with community narratives. *Journal of Public Deliberation, 15*(3), Article 6. https://www.publicdeliberation.net/jpd/vol15/iss3/art6

Carlee, R. (2019, Spring). The Arlington Way: Public engagement as a community expectation. *National Civic Review, 108* (1), 25–32.

Goodall, H. L. (2000). *Writing the new ethnography*. AltaMira.

Nabatchi, T., & Leighninger, M. (2015). *Public participation for 21st century democracy* (Ch. 2). Jossey-Bass.

Additional Resource

Jennings, C. A. (2005). *Robert's rules for dummies*. Wiley Publishing.

News Talks

Following the news gives us information, ideas, and inspiration. From learning what is happening to why events unfolded as they did, you might wonder how are people responding and how did a certain story evolve over time? Reading the newspaper provides insight into questions of local politics, state happenings, national news, and global affairs.

The newspaper and other news sources provide a basis from which to learn what your elected officials are doing, how people respond to those actions, and how recent events impact us, the more than 330 million people living in the United States together. Understandably, researchers are worried, then, about declining newspaper readership, reasoning that:

> In the absence of a local news organization, social media and internet sites often have become the default media for reading, viewing and sharing news—as well as rumor and gossip—exacerbating political, social and economic divisions in a polarized nation (Abernathy, 2020, p. 10).

Though newspaper circulation and readership are admittedly on the decline, newspapers remain a vital resource for local stories, providing residents with more crucial information than other news outlets.

> A Duke [University] study of 100 mid-sized communities in 2016 found that newspapers accounted for 60 percent of stories produced in a typical week that addressed a critical information need. By comparison, only 15 percent of the stories produced by other outlets— television, radio, and online news sites—were both locally produced and met a critical information need (Abernathy, 2020, p. 93).

When you have information about your community and its concerns, you have a foundation for conversation or news talks, which in turns provides a gateway to thinking about and taking action both alone and with others. Reading the newspaper increases your civic knowledge, enhances your ability to talk clearly about issues of the day, and deepens your understanding of how people evaluate the complexity, importance, and value of events, sometimes differently, in accordance with different ethical values. For students of communication ethics, talking about the news demonstrates how ethical perspectives play out in everyday actions.

In summary, former *Wall Street Journal* and *New York Times* executive Pamela Muse Abernathy (2020) says that local news remains a vital link to freedom of expression and civic engagement:

> The coronavirus pandemic has reminded us, yet again, of the vital importance of local news. Interest in and appreciation for local news has surged in recent months, as residents in cities and rural communities have searched for accurate, reliable and comprehensive information about what is occurring in their own neighborhood. Yet, at this very moment, local news organizations, large and small, for-profit and nonprofit, are confronting a dire economic threat to their existence. Even in their drastically diminished state, surviving local newspapers still remain a vital source of local news and information. A recent study found that local newspapers produce more than half of all original local stories that address

a critical information need—such as education, the environment and the health and safety of our community. This suggests the importance of public policy and philanthropic efforts that support the viability of strong local newspapers, as well as digital-only news outlets, ethnic media and public broadcasting. In order to replenish and revive the local news ecosystem, and address the information needs of underserved communities, there needs to be both a significant increase in funding and a recommitment to journalism's civic mission (p. 53).

With this activity, you'll increase your *knowledge* by considering:

- What ethical issues are in the news?

- How do newspapers and news outlets best serve our communities?

You'll have the opportunity to learn *skills* by considering:

- How does engaging in dialogue help you better understand the news?

- What ways, orally and in writing, can you respond to a story over time?

- How can you best read and access a newspaper?

You can consider your own *values* and that of others by asking:

- Whose perspectives are highlighted in a story and why?

- What would you say about this news issue in line with your values?

- How are local newspapers the same and different from social media news sources?

Putting what you learn into *action* means asking:

- What groups or people could you work with to advance a community initiative featured in the news?

- Who could you talk to about the news to deepen your understanding and theirs about local and community issues?

The Activity

1. Read the newspaper during the course term and select articles involving ethical issues (the number of required articles will be determined by your instructor).

2. Write several paragraphs for each article that includes a link to the article, an introduction, review of the article and issue, brief application to an ethical perspective, and two related questions about communicating ethically for your classmates to consider.

Reflection Instructions

1. Discuss your newspaper articles with others in a small group, focusing on communication ethics.

2. What questions, issues, or concerns arise using a different ethical perspective to evaluate the newspaper article?

3. Where else could you turn for information to help you deepen your understanding of the content in the newspaper article?

Reference

Abernathy, P. M. (2020). *News deserts and ghost newspapers: Will local news survive?* Center for Innovation and Sustainability in Local Media, UNC Press.

Additional Resource

Mindich, D. T. Z. (2004). *Why Americans under 40 don't follow the news.* Oxford University Press.

Voting, Elections, and Me

Voting is a necessary and defining feature of our democracy. It is often discussed as both a right and a responsibility that came for many after long-fought battles. Voting rights have continually expanded from the time our country was founded. For instance, in 1920, the 19th Amendment to the U.S. Constitution secured the right for women to vote. In 1965, President Lyndon Johnson signed the Voting Rights Act to eliminate restrictive state laws involving such things as poll taxes and literacy tests that were barriers constructed to keep African Americans, Latinos, Native Americans, and Asian Americans from voting, particularly in the South. In 1971, the 26th Amendment lowered the voting age from 21 to 18.

Though securing and keeping the right to vote has been a struggle over time, many Americans still fail to cast their ballots in federal, state, and local elections. Some argue that it's just not worth their time since corporate interests essentially buy elections with campaign contributions and heavy advertising. Others say, if we give up voting, we give up the possibility of influencing who our next leaders will be. To learn more about your upcoming elections, use the newspaper, Facebook, campaign websites, and other resources to help you identify candidates and issues that will be decided upon at the ballot box.

Voting is ethics in action. When you vote, you make choices about what you value, and your vote expresses those values. Will you vote to promote your own self-interest or is the welfare of the community your goal? Do you take justice as a starting point or are individual rights paramount? When you vote, you have the opportunity to influence the shape and complexion of our government. Will you vote for projects that may add to your tax bill as is often the case in bonds for schools or cultural arts buildings, or to lower your taxes and not support public services? How important is paying for high water quality or public transportation? Do you vote for a strong defense or a strong public education system? Do you vote for religious reasons or for pluralistic ones? Your vote helps determine whose lives in your communities are made better or worse and not just yourself. Do you want to vote for candidates that reflect the racial composition of your community? Do you think our elected officials should have gender diversity? Or do you vote to maintain the status quo (the way things are currently)? The questions you ask and the decisions you make communicate ethical perspectives as well as your own personal values. This is why politics are so heated—our core values are at stake and we want our values to be expressed. It feels personal when our issues, candidates, and ideas win or lose.

With this assignment, you'll increase your *knowledge* by considering:

- How do you research the job, responsibilities, and scope of duties associated with candidates in an upcoming election?

- How can you learn who are the candidates running for office or the ballot initiatives requiring votes?

- What are ways you can determine if sources are unbiased?

You'll have the opportunity to learn *skills* by considering:

- How can you register yourself and others to vote?

- How can you apply for an absentee ballot? Where can you vote early and when?

You can consider your own *values* and that of others by asking:

- What candidate and/or ballot item espouses the ethical values you hold as most important? Be sure to define the values by which you are judging the candidate or ballot item (you might consider justice, inclusion, government transparency, etc.).

Putting what you learn into *action* means asking:

- Which candidate for the race, or position on the ballot item you researched do you think people should vote for and why? What does this reveal about your values for your community?

- What organizations endorse the candidates and/or issue and how can you contribute to their communication efforts?

- What upcoming opportunities exist in the community to learn more about the candidates and/or issue?

The Activity

1. Since voting requirements and processes are established at the state level and carried out differently at the local level, it is important for you to understand how your home state oversees elections. Go to this website for that information: https://www.ncsl.org/research/elections-and-campaigns/election-administration-at-state-and-local-levels.aspx

2. Individually or in a small group, as directed by your instructor, research on your computer, tablet, or smartphone where people in your community can register to vote. Find out the deadlines for registering for the next election in your community, how to get a sample ballot, and the ways you can vote in the upcoming election (by mail, in person, early voting, etc.). In doing so, you're expanding your voter skills.

3. Choose an upcoming electoral race to research and write a paper detailing what you learned about the candidates, proposed amendments, bonds, or other initiatives, based on at least three sources (Facebook pages, newspaper articles, candidate websites, voter election guides, etc.). Provide answers to the questions posed above regarding *knowledge*, *values*, and *action*.

4. Discuss your research in a brief oral presentation.

Additional Resources

Broadening Youth Voting, https://circle.tufts.edu/our-research/broadening-youth-voting

Campus Compact Election Engagement Project, https://compact.org/initiatives/campus-vote-home/

Rock the Vote, https://www.rockthevote.org/

You Can Vote, www.youcanvote.org

What Free Speech Boundaries, if any, Do We Want?

When people talk about free speech or freedom of expression, does that mean we can or should say anything we want? Like most important values (and rights), the answer is not simple. Free speech as a First Amendment right means that we cannot be punished by the government for what we say (though it's important to know that there are some time and place restrictions). Our democracy in theory protects us from those who would not want us to talk about unpopular ideas or criticize the government. This protection is not one held as a universal value in other parts of the world, which makes the United States unique. At the same time, the First Amendment does not free us from the consequences of speech that might harm other citizens or institutions (like schools and businesses) nor does it give us license to say or do whatever we want. You can express your freedom of speech without fear from the government, but your employer may have other ideas, for instance.

Democracy depends on public spaces and the expression of free speech in open-air debates, club meetings, town halls, demonstrations, and rallies where people voice their hopes, dreams, or dissent toward customs, institutions, and authorities. In doing so, free speech may confront competing values surrounding morality, diversity, public safety, and notions of a just society. Yet, for all the struggles that define and emerge from free speech, we continue to protect its prominence as a cherished American freedom.

Some argue that since the First Amendment encourages us to seek truth and liberty without fear of punishment or government restrictions, we must tolerate hate speech and racist discourse. Others argue that our speech should be self-monitored to uphold respect and dignity for all people. In response to the practical difficulty of distinguishing the boundaries of hate speech, the U.S. Supreme Court has ruled repeatedly that such restrictions would suppress the public debate that democracy requires.

© Spoma Jovanovic

We know that tolerating hate speech, speech that intentionally demeans the value of other human beings, not only hurts the individuals to whom the speech is targeted, but also undermines a foundational equality principle as stated in the Declaration of Independence, namely that all people (not only men) are created equal.

We are living in a time where people are speaking up, as demonstrated in our cities and around the world recently by young people taking charge of conversations for police accountability, climate justice, immigration reform, and the elimination of school gun violence, to name just a few of the topics around which they have galvanized wide support.

To stand up and speak out in the public sphere requires courage and persistence in the face of inevitable resistance, dismissiveness, rudeness, and sometimes even threatening responses. Thus, all of us, students, teachers, community members, elected leaders, and judges, need to ask what are the tasks we need to undertake as part of our evolving standards of creating an ethical, just world? How do our cherished ideals of free speech, equality for all, and democracy best operate together? It is clear from our community actions that we are never far from debates and disputes over the scope and meaning of how speech can and should be used in public spaces.

On college campuses, for example, when, if ever should speakers be disinvited or prevented from being on campus? Or, under what conditions, if any, should we insist on safe spaces and/or trigger warnings to protect students? How should we respond to hate speech on campuses? Why has taking a knee during the national anthem elicited both support and outrage?

In our communities, people have considered whether stepping on the American Flag as a teaching moment is prudent, even if it is a protected right. They have also discussed panhandling, and asked is begging for money protected free speech? Is it different from unsolicited requests for donations? How and why? Others have talked about pornography. Is it art that falls under freedom of expression? Or does it unduly and immorally objectify and subjugate women?

In this activity, you'll increase your *knowledge* by thinking about:

- What is permissible according to the First Amendment and what are its limits?

- What different speech responses are best surrounding a public issue and why?

You can consider your *values* and that of others by asking:

- How do you balance the legal protections afforded to free speech with a consideration of other legal protections and ethical obligations?

- Who benefits most and who bears the burdens most from free speech?

- How does limiting free speech express certain values of the United States?

Putting what you learn into *action* means asking:

- How and where can you speak out on an issue?

- What actions can you take to communicate ethically on issues with which you may or may not agree?

The Activity

First, get a little background information by reading Chemerinsky and Gillam's (2018) article, "The Various Threat to Free Speech on Campus" that appeared in the March 2018 issue of NCA's *Spectra* Magazine (https://www.natcom.org/publications/spectra/march-2018). Then, locate and read about a free speech issue of concern to you. Following that, write a statement that identifies the free speech concern, what ethics and communication might suggest, and your views about the demands and limits of free speech.

Tips for organizing your paper:

1. Use the introduction to detail the free speech concern. Provide enough details so the reader understands the background and current state of affairs.

2. Detail what ethical perspectives/theories and issues you have considered and why.

3. Conclude with a discussion of how ethics and legal protections should be weighed in this case to assert your view.

Reference

Chemerinsky, E., & Gillam, H. (2018, March). The various threats to free speech on campus. *Spectra: The Magazine of the National Communication Association, 54*(1), 14–18.

Additional Resources

Arnett, R. C. (1990). The practical philosophy of communication ethics and free speech as the foundation for speech communication. *Communication Quarterly, 38*(3), 208–217.

Chemerinsky, E., & Gillman, H. (2017). *Free speech on campus.* Yale University Press.

Social Movements

Social movements are large-scale, grassroots efforts by everyday people to invoke changes in behaviors, norms, and laws that are central to democratic life. A social movement is defined by the collective energy and momentum that arise after years of relationship building and organizing efforts among groups, associations, and loosely knit networks to address what they consider to be injustices in public life. These movements often depend upon protests and marches to make their claims visible, but their actions include so much more, including meeting in homes to discuss strategies and tactics, lobbying local, state, and federal officials, initiating legal challenges, hosting potluck events to recruit and sustain supporters, and proposing policy changes. As people gather to imagine a world different from the one they inhabit now, they create a vision of new possibilities. At the same time, activists and organizers in social movements often use vitriolic communication designed specifically to arouse public concern and express dissent toward the powerful forces operating to discredit efforts for change.

A historical look at social movements reveals that their successes are dependent upon moral suasion (i.e., persuasion) that is expressed in the communication and coordinated action by collectives to resist or correct injustices in social, political, cultural, and economic arenas. Unfortunately, traditional textbooks often leave out or minimize the impact of these movements. Just a few examples of social movements in history that have influenced how we live today include:

Women's Suffrage, United States, 1848–1920: To secure the right for women to vote in elections.

Salt March, India, 1930: Led by Gandhi in protest over British rule in India.

Civil Rights, United States, 1955–1968: To gain equal rights for Black Americans.

United Farm Workers, United States, 1962–1972: For improved working conditions in agriculture.

Vietnam Draft Resistance, United States, 1965–1972: Protests against mandatory armed services enlistment.

Americans with Disabilities, United States, 1973–1990: To build infrastructure and policies necessary to accommodate people with disabilities.

Three Mile Island Anti-Nuclear, United States, 1979–1985: Action to regulate and reduce use of nuclear power.

Tiananmen Square, China, 1989: Pro-democracy and freedom movement led by students.

Apartheid Divestiture, South Africa, 1969–1987: Campaign to eliminate foreign investments where a system of racial segregation persisted.

MeToo Movement, United States, 2006–2018: To empower victims of sexual harassment and abuse.

Occupy Wall Street, United States, 2011–2016: Protests against economic inequities between the wealthiest 1% and the remaining 99% of the people.

Arab Spring, Egypt, 2011–2012: Protests fueled by social media against an oppressive, authoritarian political regime.

Black Lives Matter, United States, since 2013: A comprehensive program to affirm the humanity of Black lives in the face of deadly oppression.

Umbrella Revolution, Hong Kong, 2014: Uprising to demand that people select future leaders, rather than cede control to China.

Brexit, United Kingdom, 2016–2020: A struggle over whose voices were valid in the United Kingdom's withdrawal from the European Union.

Women's March, United States, since 2017: A women led, nonviolent movement to advance collective liberation.

Yellow Vests, France, 2018–2020: Grassroots resistance movement advocating for economic justice.

Hong Kong Protests, China, 2019–2020: Protests against extradition bill that would subject Hong Kong residents to unfair trials and violent treatment by China.

What an important impact these social movements have had in leading toward justice! For example, we wouldn't have environmental protections or LGBTQ rights without them. We wouldn't have regular workdays limited to 8 hours a day or child labor protection laws. By studying these movements, you will learn how people like you have spoken and acted in concert with their ethics in collective action. The more you learn the history of these movements, the more it will become clear how current-day movements are relevant to you.

Social movements use many approaches to amplify their messages with campaigns that may include one or more of the following: petitions, posters, bumper stickers, living-room meetings, film showings, street painting, leaflets and brochures, mass meetings, rallies, protests, social media blasts, staged newsworthy events, strikes, speeches, and civil disobedience to name a few (Bowers et al., 2010).

In this activity, you'll increase your *knowledge* by thinking about:

- What is a social movement and how is it connected to communication ethics?

- How can we change our communities to make them more just?

You'll have the opportunity to learn new *skills* by considering:

- What writing and speaking strategies and skills do social movements use?

You can consider your *values* and that of others by asking:

- How are the values of people involved in social movements reflected in the ways the movement communicates in flyers, posters, manifestos, social media, and/or brochures?

- How are the values of people involved in social movements often belittled, ignored, or overlooked, and what unethical strategies do opponents use to do so?

Putting what you learn into *action* means asking:

- What new and creative ways could you use to communicate ethically today that may not have been available to past social movements?

- What advantages and disadvantages do new communication forms have over traditional modes of outreach?

The Activity

This is a research paper designed for you to pursue your interests in learning more about how one past social movement led to change, relying on ethical communication to achieve its goals.

Part I: Research a social movement of your choice. Provide some detail of the movement's messages or rhetoric, the people driving the action (who they were as a group), the counter forces that made the work challenging, and the outcomes.

Part II: Provide an analysis of the social movement that considers how the communication advanced an ethical stance. Be sure to consider the written and oral messages of the movement and its goals. You might critically examine the mission of the movement, for instance, or recruiting materials. Use the class readings to help you in the analysis (making meaningful connections between your research and the readings).

Part III: Conclude with some creative suggestions of your own for how to improve the movement if you were to launch it today (recognizing that conditions are somewhat different, yet maybe similar).

Reference

Bowers, J. W., Ochs, D. J., Jensen, R. J., & Schulz, D. P. (2010). *The rhetoric of agitation and control* (3rd ed.). Waveland Press.

Additional Resources

DelGandio, J. (2008). *Rhetoric for radicals*. New Society Publishers.

Morris, C. E., & Browne, S. H. (2013). *Readings on the rhetoric of social protest* (3rd ed.). Strata Publishing.

Zinn, H. (2003). *A people's history of the United States*. Harper Perennial Modern Classics.

Reading: *Communication, Dialogue, and Student Activism* by Spoma Jovanovic

STUDENTS, BY THE nature of their roles as students, ask questions. One question that sometimes takes a bit of time to form, but eventually emerges as they learn of collective actions making headlines, such as the women's march or the Black Lives Matter movement, is, "Where and how do social change processes start?" The follow-up question they pose is perhaps the more important one: "How do social change movements persist against the backdrop of threats, criticisms, and worse?"

The answers to these questions can be found in the work and impact of ordinary people, to whom we owe a debt for the myriad progressive reforms they have championed throughout history. Yet, in many, if not most educational settings, the lessons to be gleaned from involved, knowledgeable citizens have been largely omitted from formal teaching, leaving too many students without important history and classroom instruction to help them become active participants in promoting justice in our democracy (Zinn, 2015). Imagine if our youth in elementary school, high school, and college discussed the ways in which people have confronted the roots of racial injustice, gender inequality, labor struggles for fair wages and working conditions, immigration policies, and the long overdue corrections required to combat disabilities discrimination. Imagine how students could learn to discern important facts and values in those conversations that bring history alive by learning about collective action efforts.

Activist history, too often maligned for its trouble-making qualities and sidelined from mainstream academic instruction, deserves to be lifted up for the lessons and skills it provides to students. Such knowledge allows students to build and improve on the work of people who dared to challenge injustices where they existed in favor of a more compassionate, equitable, and fair world. Activists, in this country and around the globe, join together to advocate for a world where we are connected in "a community woven together from sharing and mutual care; a community of concern and responsibility for the equal right to be human and the equal ability to act on that right" (Bauman, 1998, p. 150).

Activist history, in addition to providing essential political and contextual grounding, necessarily examines how communication is the ethical expression of our humanity that emerges as the most essential resource for social change. It is communication that builds enduring relationships vital to every broad-based movement. It is through our interactions that we learn to include and appreciate multiple perspectives as an avenue for bridging differences, which is so necessary for democracy. Communication propels us to express our care for others and invite deliberation on important decision making. Indeed, "Language is one of the most potent resources each of us has for achieving our own political empowerment" (Allen, 2014, p. 22). Communication is the starting point for learning of, talking about, and remedying through social change the struggles, discrimination, and unfairness others have faced. It is educational work that is rewarding, fulfilling, and meaningful.

Of the many invaluable peak experiences in school, at the top of the list often cited by my former students are the times when they met new people of different cultures or when they engaged in discussions about social, political, and economic issues, or when they discovered previously unknown stories and histories that activated a desire to make the world better. When education serves as midwife to democracy's realization in everyday life (Dewey, 2008), the learning experience is transformed from a passive consideration of disconnected facts into an active, robust space where students exchange ideas and investigate the means by which we can all live together peacefully and productively. In that vibrant setting, educators can introduce students to stories and present-day experiences that demonstrate how profound community change arises from the collective action of people to influence other constituents, including government officials and community groups.

This chapter offers an overview of challenges to democracy that influence the modes and means of inspiring student activism through communication and drawing on the resources embedded in dialogue, public deliberation, collective action, and protest events. There is renewed interest to encourage student voting and political participation after decades of decline (CIRCLE, 2008); thus the time is right for a deep consideration of and teaching about the many forms of democratic expression vital for ensuring a strong democracy. When students can discern the various routes to activism and see themselves as part of a rich history, they will learn how to join people—one, two, three and more at a time—to introduce new ideas powerful enough to move minds, hearts, policies, and laws.

21st-Century Challenges

In the 21st century, students are familiar with crises that are rife with moral consequences. Students feel the impact of climate change conversations, economic downturns, calls for police accountability, assaults on voting rights, and escalating gun violence in schools. They see as well both the robust and feeble attempts by their elected leaders to mitigate the impacts of these calamities and the grassroots organizers who often pose alternative solutions. If we are lucky, we see students' ethical sensibilities awaken as they consider their roles and responsibilities in the controversies.

Students have witnessed the devastating impact of environmental disasters on historically underrepresented communities. In 2005, Hurricane Katrina shed light on how policies of the Army Corp of Engineers contributed to the disaster that flooded New Orleans, leaving more than one-quarter of the city's residents in dire straits, particularly those who were poor and without transportation to evacuate as ordered. Five years later, in 2010, the unprecedented British Petroleum (BP) oil spill off the Gulf Coast generated public outrage and action over unchecked drilling practices. Following a United States District Court ruling that BP was guilty of gross negligence and reckless conduct, the company agreed to pay $18.7 billion in fines, the largest corporate settlement in U.S. history. Students notice these predicaments, care about them, and in some cases take action. For other students, the situations described here seem beyond their reach to do anything worthwhile.

Economic declines, too, have made headlines repeatedly, impacting the opportunities and hopes students could consider. The recession of 2007 implicated criminal banking practices that led to record bankruptcies, home foreclosures, and plummeting savings accounts. Corporate greed was at the root of the problem. It lined the pockets of financial executives but left the cookie jars of ordinary people empty. Students—most of whom fell into the 99%, which the Occupy Wall Street worked to bring attention to—wondered how such an economic disaster could happen and how the top 1% of the nation's wealthy could continue to amass fortunes while their families lost ground. For the first time in our country's history, these students were among those who would likely have a future less secure than the previous generation (Allison, 2017). Students learned at a tender young age that their elders were not going to be able to ensure a more prosperous future.

Police practices have also galvanized student attention as unarmed Black people were killed, often without provocation, shocking a nation that witnessed so many of the events on cellular phone footage. Trayvon Martin (2012), Miriam Carey (2013), Tamir Rice (2014), Eric Garner (2014), Michael Brown (2014), Walter Scott (2015), and Keith Lamont Scott (2016) were just a few of the country's citizens who lost their lives at the hands of the police, along with 266 unarmed Black people in 2016 alone, according to *The Guardian's* interactive tracking system (2017). Students responded with protests and despair. Three young women did more. In response to what they considered a state-sanctioned attack on Black people, the three started Black Lives Matter in 2013 to call attention to the crisis in modem militaristic police action.

Voting rights have been under renewed assault in the 21st century, prompting rage and action of faith-based and community groups. From the Moral Monday movement in North Carolina (Schradie, 2018) that galvanized a multi-racial, multi-generational alliance to lawsuits filed against gerrymandering around the country to protests against required photo identification in the voting booth, students were often put in the middle of the controversy. In some states, parents were threatened with legal action and fines if their college-bound students voted outside their hometown precincts. In other locales, student voting booths on or near schools were eliminated in an attempt to limit the influence of student voices (Liebelson, 2014).

Students would not be silent, however, as gun violence in schools escalated, which started with the 1999 Columbine Massacre in Littleton, Colorado, that left 15 dead and 24 wounded. Since then, according to the *Washington Post*, more than 150,000 students attending at least 170 U.S. schools have been victims of gun violence on their campuses (Rozsa, Balingit, Wan, & Berman, 2018). In the aftermath of the most tragic and visible of the shootings, including Virginia Tech in 2007, Sandy Hook Elementary in 2012, and Marjory Stoneman Douglas High School in 2018, parents and other activists have called for comprehensive gun reform. However, most efforts for meaningful change stalled until the Parkland, Florida, teenagers at Marjory Stoneman Douglas High School turned their grief into activism with their campaign, # never-again. Within three weeks of their unyielding, coordinated effort to march on Washington, lobby state officials, coordinate national walkouts, and respond to media interviews, Florida signed into law new gun safety legislation. Florida raised the minimum age for buying guns to 21, mandated a waiting period for gun purchases, and provided funding for increased school security and mental health services (Astor, 2018). Though the bill did not achieve all the goals the Florida teenagers advocated for, it was the first successful gun reform in that state in more than 20 years. More importantly, the work of those teenagers launched a national conversation in defiance of the well-funded political influence wielded by the National Rifle Association.

Of note is that all these crises have taken place amidst a declining faith in democracy, not only in the United States, but also worldwide, according to leading researchers of democratic governance: "The public spheres of informed and engaged citizens seem to be weakening across countries, even in those with well-functioning media landscapes and relatively high levels of political awareness and participation" (Anheier, 2017, p. 15). In thinking of how to better care for democracy, scholars increasingly point to our youth as the ones on whom we must rely to disrupt the status quo in favor of transformational change needed to enhance citizen engagement, improve institutional practices within government, and effect a culture shift that results in people more deeply discussing and debating the fate of our future.

Still, student activism faces its own challenges. Increasingly, the noble views of responsible citizenship have slipped away with the fervor of consumerism taking root in its place to relegate education as simply a by-product of market-driven values (Giroux, 2012). Absent concerted instruction on what it means to be an involved person in the community—one who can effect change for the good—this most recent generation of college students finds itself asking, "What can I do?" These students wonder how it is possible that the most basic of human needs—health care, employment benefits, a living wage, public education, and voting rights—seem to be dwindling before their eyes. Critical educator Richard Brosio (2017) says teachers often are complicit in hegemonic conceptions of education beholden to market-based capitalism despite the national call to provide more civically engaged studies:

> The capitalist economic imperative requests that the schools produce competent, willing workers; whereas, the democratic-egalitarian imperative requests that public education develop critical, well-rounded citizen-workers who are committed to complex roles beyond work—and who may use their critical skills to analyze capitalists work relations, and command of the economy, (p. 569)

Thus, schooling itself is a contested site, where students are compelled through their studies to uphold the hierarchy and inequities that are pervasive in society while also (sometimes, though not often enough) being asked to question and challenge the injustices they witness.

Ensuring the health and vibrancy of our democracy requires an entire community's effort, to be sure, but there are many, many small and large projects contributing to this goal that are most often started by just a few. It only requires a handful of people who are persistent and clear in their vision to provide the opportunity for more people to be included in determining their collective fate. Admittedly, the elected establishment and even school administrators may not (always) agree with the creative and courageous actions inspired by "people power." Those leaders may even resist the intrusions, but students are often wise to join with ordinary people struggling simply to secure the most basic human rights. Despite the racism, economic exploitation, gender inequities, and other persistent injustices—or perhaps because of them—students can gain a sense of the moral outrage worthy of pause and applause (Purpel, 1999).

Speaking Out: Modes and Means of Inspiring Activism

Social change begins with a conversation or dialogue among people who care about an issue in their community. Their talk proceeds to decision making about what to do next, oftentimes transforming disparate conversations into a spirited story of the need to right an injustice. Next, organizing efforts intensify to expand partnerships and build momentum among not a few, but many, people. Finally, the work culminates with speaking out through varied actions to achieve a new vision.

The pattern for advancing positive social change is there, and the examples are easy to locate among the activist communities. The challenge for educators is to make those activist stories widely available to the uninitiated. Faculty can provide important learning experiences for students by including social change readings in the curriculum, inviting community leaders into the classroom, pushing students to do research and take action with the community, and in other ways bridging course content to activism so students can understand fully how social change happens and how academic studies provide a strong basis for students to contribute to communities' efforts for change.

Dialogue

For activists—students and community members alike—conversations that matter revolve around and reflect political matters. As James Baldwin (1963) said in his famous "A Talk to

Teachers," "The obligation of anyone who thinks of himself as responsible is to examine society and try to change it and to fight it—at no matter what risk (p. 42). The starting point is in having a conversation that serves to illuminate injustices worthy of intervention.

Throughout history, we see many examples of how dialogic moments provided the impetus for protracted struggle leading to important social change. For instance, the battle to secure women's right to vote was won in 1920 with the ratification of the Nineteenth Amendment to the U.S. Constitution, more than 70 years after conversations about that needed change began at the landmark Seneca Falls Convention in New York in 1848 (Williams, 2009). The 8-hour workday was standardized and implemented into federal law by the Fair Labor Standards Act in 1937, based on conversations Philadelphia carpenters had in 1791 that continued in various forms and fashion for 146 years before culminating in a labor victory (King, 2004). We applaud now the value of the American Disabilities Act that was enacted in 1990, but students need to know that the conversations and advocacy for people who had been institutionalized and systematically from their communities spanned over five decades (Krahn, Walker, & Correa-De-Araujo, 2015).

Though time intensive, dialogue that emerges in conversations provides important spaces and occasions for people to engage deeply with one another, reflecting on new voices and views that can lead to fresh understandings. Philosopher Martin Buber (1970) noted that dialogue is a critical feature of public life demarcated by a recognition of others as unique, complete beings. For Buber, dialogue is steeped in authenticity, not obfuscation, and respect for the other, not command or control of the other. Mikhail Bakhtin further considered dialogue as a multivocal rendering of the human condition in which our own voice is moderated and strengthened by the words and utterances of others (1986).

Dialogue in the classroom is the critical first step needed to activate student voices. Doing so requires handing over time and control to students to engage in talk that reveals their values, beliefs, and understanding of the world. Dialogue is an inclusive pedagogical practice that communicates to students that they are active participants in their own learning, rather than passive receptors of information (Freire, 1992). By engaging in dialogue in the classroom, students experience communication as a collaborative method by which to demonstrate mutual commitment, even when the dialogue predictably becomes uncomfortable. Alphonso Lingis (1994) says it is precisely when we are feeling exposed and vulnerable in the presence of another that a sense of community can emerge. Within these genuine relationships, rather than ones predetermined by power dynamics and roles we assume in society, dialogue becomes the medium by which students can reach new understanding (Makau & Marty, 2013). That is, conversations allow us to build and sustain positive relationships in the community. It is a collective task for which we all have a stake and a responsibility (Jovanovic, 2012). It is through dialogue that people can start to imagine and give words to better ideas that alone they may not have been able to conceive. Once a new understanding emerges, the next step is deliberation wherein students make decisions about what needs to be the focus of their action steps.

Deliberation

Activism of any sort in a democracy depends on coordinated action, communication, and decision making among people, which accommodates their diverse voices. Public deliberation, then, is the process by which we can "carefully examine a problem and arrive at a well-reasoned solution after a period of inclusive, respectful consideration of diverse points of view" (Gastil, 2008, p. 8).

Making deliberation practical in our democracy rests on four requirements of equality: inclusion of different voices; thoughtfulness or genuine consideration of competing claims and arguments; the ability to impact the larger public conversation; and, finally, open and trusting social and political conditions in which deliberations can take place (Fishkin, 2009). Deliberation, thus, thrives on dissenting views as much as it does on the ethical commitment to stay engaged with others in the hopes of arriving at the most just solutions possible.

It would be difficult to find a more perfect arena in which to practice both dialogue and deliberation than a college classroom. There, diversity abounds as students enter with varied backgrounds, experiences, and cultural identities. They are not brought together under the guise of shared backgrounds, as is the case for most social situations in life. Students, in fact, often find themselves for the first time coming face to face with people different from them in virtually every way. While disparities in wealth define many social relations that in turn limit the participation and possibilities of public deliberation (Swartz, Campbell, & Pestana, 2009), there are fewer of those inequalities in the college classroom. Still, critical pedagogues would argue that our educational institutions, policies, and practices continue to reward privileged students (Oakes, Lipton, Anderson, & Stillman, 2018). So, while the college classroom provides a glorious space for students to explore new ideas and heretofore unknown facts, a critical orientation is needed to support the development of activism. Considering the history and conditions that give rise to current educational practices is one way to do so, as well as weighing current socio-political concerns. When students are granted the opportunity for meaningful communication, they encounter each other as worthy colleagues in the struggle over what "ought we to do" in advancing justice in our democracy (Mouffe, 2000).

Deliberation requires adjudicating among competing claims. In the classroom, we point to critical thinking as the pedagogical tool for teaching students how to examine, critique, and defend claims based on facts, history, reasons, stories, and other evidence. Just as necessary is teaching students to recognize their own and others' belief systems that shape how we see and understand the world. By being attentive to how these larger worldviews influence talk and decision making, students can be better prepared to address obstacles to deliberative processes and framing of the issues under consideration (Makau & Marty, 2013).

Ernesto Cortes (2007) reminds us that our democracy was built on conflict, and thus we need to teach students skills for argumentation and deliberation for them to consider the options surrounding contentious public issues so that they can reach good decisions. To do so, students need to learn their disciplinary content, but they also need to develop the capacities to engage, question, argue, interpret, and contextualize experiences and encounters sufficient to challenge authority when needed. Doing so in tandem with others offers the greatest opportunity for success.

Collective Action

Just as cooperative learning is designed to improve learning outcomes, collective action is intended to coalesce disparate voices to improve the chances of securing social change. The parallels between cooperative learning and collective action are noteworthy. First, both rely on students working together to solve a problem, investigate a concept, and propose solutions. Second, both have increased chances of success when participants inject themselves fully into the process with open-mindedness and creative thinking. Third, when students recognize the power they have to effect change in the classroom and in the community, they are more likely to accept greater responsibility and leadership in future actions.

Marshall Ganz, former farmworker organizer, civil rights activist, and consultant to President Barack Obama's 2008 grassroots campaign efforts, now advocates in his role as a professor for students to consider the merits of organizing through relationship building, developing common understanding, and taking action (Ganz, 2010). Ganz affirms the power of dialogue to deepen understanding and relationships among people strong enough to withstand inevitable frustrations and questioning that arise from allies and opponents. Dialogue and deliberation teach students confidence. Collective action teaches students that there are others on their side, ready to support them and stand with them. With those essential competencies in place, students can first prepare to assert a voice interconnected to one another to perhaps address smaller objectives to see how progress toward a larger goal is possible.

Stories are powerful ways to organize others toward a social change goal. Stories provide a conversational base to encourage understanding and build community. Undocumented youth, for instance, use their stories as a political tool in the face of deportation to touch people's hearts:

> Dreamers who came out transformed themselves from stereotypes or projections into fleshed-out characters with wounds and hopes and universal values. . . . Increasingly, social movement strategists and leaders from across the spectrum—from immigration rights to marriage equality to climate justice—are making narrative a core part of their strategy. (Moe, 2004, p. 47)

Students who share and listen to stories anchored in powerful experiences and connected to structural problems find their imaginations soar to connect with others as a base for collective action.

Strengthening civic participation in this way entails, as well, three other elements: empowering and activating leaders and networks, assembling varied participation building blocks, and offering systemic supports (Nabatchi & Leighninger, 2015). That is, teachers need to tap into the potential of student leaders in their classes and support them in convening other students to reach out to community leaders and organizations. Teachers and students together can look to websites, social media, apps, and games as newer participation mediums. Finally, educators need to consider what supports they can offer to students to foster activist identity development. To do this important work, teachers might reasonably ask, "Who can we introduce students to within our colleges and universities where they will be warmly received and nurtured in activism? How can we likewise introduce students to community members engaged in advocacy work so that students can join a solid support structure to help them deepen their learning about activism?"

Speaking Out Through Protest and Other Actions

Once students have learned about an issue through in-depth dialogue and discussion, deliberated the merits of various positions, and organized collectively around a common approach to tackling injustice, the work turns toward speaking out, starting or joining protests, leading petition drives, attending legislative action committees, and in other ways confronting what requires change in visible ways.

Leading up to and engaging in speaking out benefits from the support, encouragement, and guidance of teachers, who themselves are learned and practiced in such forms of activism. This way of teaching advances *parrhesia* or free speech and fearless speech (Foucault, 2001), Epicureans in Greek times steered students to self-discovery of the truth by dialogic means in the hopes that students would in turn develop the courage to speak out publicly (Foucault, 2001). This guidance requires, among other instruction, the retelling of stories of success and failure to offer students a glimpse into the challenging work that undergirds the spectacle of many protest actions. Too often, students assume that marches and sit-ins are designed only to gain media attention. They assume that protests and marches are absent in the infrastructure required to gain traction in solving real problems. Those students are sometimes correct in their assessment; however, more often their views have been shaped by the dominant culture that caricatures dissent. When students learn from community organizers that protests are only one leg of a much larger strategy, they can better reflect on the varied options social change agents use in their work. With that knowledge in hand, students can discuss, deliberate, choose directions, and then prioritize certain actions at certain times designed to achieve specified results within a much broader program for change.

Communicating as an activist is a vehicle for self-realization and fulfillment when students are afforded authentic and genuinely equal opportunities to participate (Chafe, 1980). Indeed, amplifying our voices is more important than ever in a society where there is a cacophony of distracting messages created to keep students from understanding injustices, questioning assumptions and power relations, asserting the need for change, and taking action! This is not new. Fannie Lou Hamer recognized as much in her work as a civil rights activist. Her formal schooling ended at the age of 12, but that did not stop her from learning all she could to advance the rights of people. As an adult, she was badly beaten during the summer of 1962 when she worked to encourage voter registration in the South. Hamer again did not stop her activism, and for the next 15 years she traveled around the country telling her stories of growing up poor and Black to willing audiences. Her most notable speech was delivered at the 1964 Democratic National Convention, but in every one of her speeches, Hamer sought to empower people to recognize their own potential for activism. In 1964, Hamer offered this admonition to a Mississippi audience:

> I don't want to hear you say, "Honey, I'm behind you." Well move, I don't want you back there. Because you could be two hundred miles behind. I want you to say, "I'm with you." And we'll go up this freedom road together. (Hamer, 2011, p. 56)

Hamer was clear in proclaiming the critical need to continue cultivating activism as a logical response to persistent injustices.

Conclusion

Raising a fist. Wearing a hoodie. Taking a knee during the national anthem. Voting. Signing a petition. Participating in a march. Protesting. Boycotting. Organizing a candlelight vigil. Attending a forum, conference, teach-in, or meeting. Joining a group. Sponsoring a program, Starting a movement. Disrupting public order. These examples of student activism, evident today and in the past, are fueled by the passion to right what are seen as wrongs in the world. The staging of spectacular events may be the most visible manifestation of student activism, but the most enduring feature of the planning, implementation, and aftermath of such action is sustained dialogue.

As students navigate their higher education journey, they do so in tandem with world events. Local and global disruptions surface the inequities and injustices that persist. For many students, exposure to discussions and analyses of these events in classroom settings is often their first introduction to meaningful civic and political engagement. Professors, teachers, mentors, and college staff thus have an opportunity and responsibility to educate for democracy by introducing the varied modes of response to these critical local and world affairs (American Association of Colleges & Universities [AAC&U], 2018).

Communication is at the center of realizing the American dream; not the dream of accumulation and wealth or making it to the top, but rather the dream of equity, justice, inclusion, care, and commitment to the general welfare of all so that together we can address the lingering needs in our communities. Teachers who recognize the value of communication and dialogue in democratic pedagogy tap into the synergy of education, community activists, and student interest in ways that bring forward the gifts and resources of all together.

In doing so, students learn to situate their own power as an ethical responsibility. For too long and in too many ways, power has been exercised to subvert the potential of meaningful, positive social change. A view of challenging power presented throughout this chapter is one that is nimble, yet forceful and productive in expression through speech, public demonstrations, and more informal conversations.

The cornerstone values of our First Amendment of free speech and freedom to assemble are ones teachers can introduce to students to inspire them to follow in the footsteps of those who sacrificed their time and energy to ensure democracy for all. Our cultural and historical roots point to people, who time and again offered conversational openings as a starting point for activism. That offer, to invite others into solidarity around a public concern, starts with the welcome, a communicative act that reflects a responsibility for the other as an ethical imperative (Levinas, 1998).

Leading critical pedagogue Henry Giroux concurs, as this chapter has espoused, that for student activism to become an education priority as insurance for protecting the future of our democracy, communication, and more specifically, dialogue, should be at the center of our instruction. He says:

> Making the political more pedagogical means treating students as critical agents; making knowledge problematic and open to debate; engaging in critical and thoughtful dialogue; and making the case for a qualitatively better world for all people. (Giroux, 2017, p. 632)

Teachers need to teach important modes and means of inspiring activism. They need to infuse history lessons into current debates and to foreground the important work of social change agents in the past. Doing so will allow today's students to see themselves as active agents in a legacy of struggle for justice. Zygmunt Bauman (1988) rightly defined the project of reclaiming democracy and our sense of community as that which offers equality of resources for all in ways that can prevail even in the face of individual incapacities and misfortunes.

Our communicative practices define our values, and they need to be nurtured inside and out of the classroom to best prepare students to tap into the possibilities of speaking with others, collaborating, and engaging in cooperative ventures for the purpose of advancing social justice. Talking across difference offers that critical opportunity to bridge the divide in social capital that too often keeps us apart by race, social class, religion, socio-economic status, political affiliations, and professional identities. Further, teachers need to teach students to recognize that difference, and even conflict, are not deterrents to, but instead sources of energy for, meaningful community action. Conversations strong enough to change the cultural narrative will not start by seeking consensus, but instead will require courage to illuminate where democracy has fallen short of its ideals and where democracy is needed most.

From *Student Activism in the Academy*. Reproduced with permission of Myers Education Press.

References

AAC&U. (2018). *We aspire: Advancing student performance through integration, research, and excellence.* Available from https://www.aacu.org/about/strategicplan

Allen, D. (2014). *Our declaration: A reading of the Declaration of Independence in defense of equality.* New York, NY: Liveright.

Allison, T. (2017, January). Financial health of young America: Measuring generational declines between baby boomers and millennials. Washington, DC: Young Invincibles. Available from http://younginvincibles.org/reports-briefs/financial-health-young-america/

Anheier, H. K. (2017). Democracy challenged. In *The governance report 2017* (pp. 13–20). Oxford, UK: Oxford University.

Astor, M. (2018, March 8). Florida gun bill: What's in it and what isn't. *New York Times.* Available from https://www.nytimes.com/2018/03/08/us/florida-gun-bill.html

Bakhtin, M. (1986). *Speech genres and other late essays* (C. Emerson & M. Holquist, Eds.; V. W. McGee, Trans.). Austin, TX: University of Texas Press.

Baldwin, J. (1963, December 21). A talk to teachers. *The Saturday Review,* pp. 42–44.

Bauman, Z. (1998). *Community: Seeking safety in an insecure world.* Cambridge, UK: Polity Press.

Brosio, R. A. (2017). The continuing conflicts between capitalism and democracy: Ramifications for schooling-education. In A. Darder, R.D. Torres, & M. P. Baltodano (Eds.), *The critical pedagogy reader* (3rd ed.) (pp. 565–577). New York, NY: Routledge.

Buber, M. (1970). *I and thou* (W. Kaufman, Trans.). New York, NY: Touchstone.

Chafe, W. (1980). *Civilities and civil rights. Greensboro, North Carolina, and the Black struggle for freedom.* New York, NY: Oxford University Press.

CIRCLE. (2008, February), *Young voter registration and turnout trends.* Available from http://civicyouth.org/PopUps/CIRCLE_RtV_Young_Voter_Trends.pdf

Cortes, E. (2007). Quality education as a civil' right: Reflections. In T. Perry, R. P. Moses, J. T. Wynne, E. Cortes, & L. Delpit (Eds.), *Quality education as a constitutional right* (pp. 93–105). Boston, MA: Beacon Press.

Dewey, J. (2008). *The school and society.* New York, NY: Cosimo Classics. (Original work published 1899)

Fishkin, J. S. (2009). *When the people speak: Deliberative democracy and public consultation.* New York, NY: Oxford University Press.

Foucault, M. (2001). *Fearless speech* (J. Pearson, Ed.). Los Angeles, CA: Semiotext(e).

Freire, P. (1992): *Pedagogy of the oppressed* (M. B. Ramos, Trans.). New York, NY: Continuum. (Original work published 1970)

Ganz, M. (2010). Leading change: Leadership, organization, and social movements. In N. Nohria & R. Khurana (Eds.), *Handbook of leadership theory and practice* (pp. 527–568). Boston, MA: Harvard University Press.

Gastil, J. (2008). *Political communication and deliberation.* Thousand Oaks, CA; SAGE,

Giroux, H. A. (2012). *Twilight of the social: Resurgent publics in the age of disposability.* Boulder, CO: Paradigm.

Giroux, H. A. (2017). Afterword: The war against teachers as public intellectuals. In A. Darder, R. D. Torres, & M. P. Baltodano (Eds.), *The critical pedagogy reader* (3rd ed.) (pp. 625–635). New York, NY: Routledge.

The Guardian (2017). The counted: People killed by the police in the US. Available from https://www.theguardian.com/us-news/ng-interactive/2015/jun/01/the-counted-police-killings-us-database.

Hamer, F. L. (2011). We're on our way: Speech delivered at a mass meeting in Indianola, Mississippi, September, 1964. In M. P. Brooks & D.W. Houck (Eds.), *The speeches of Fannie Lou Hamer: To tell it like it is* (pp. 46–56). Jackson, MI: University of Mississippi Press.

Jovanovic, S. (2012). *Democracy, dialogue, and community action: Truth and reconciliation in Greensboro.* Fayetteville, AR: Arkansas University Press.

King, B. A. (2004). Eight-hour day movement. In N. Schlager (Ed.), *St. James encyclopedia of labor history worldwide* (Vol. 1) (pp. 255–259). Detroit, MI: St, James Press.

Krahn, G. L., Walker, D. K., & Correa-De-Araujo, R. (2015). Persons with disabilities as an unrecognized health disparity population. *American Journal of Public Health, 105*(S2), 198–206.

Levinas, E. (1998). *Otherwise than being: Or beyond essence* (A. Lingis, Trans.). Pittsburgh, PA: Duquesne University Press. (Original work published 1981)

Liebelson, D. (2014, October 23). North Carolina fights to take voting site away from peaky college kids. *Huffington Post.* Available from https://www.huffingtonpost.com/2014/10/23/north-carolina-early-voting-college_n_6031670.html

Lingis, A. (1994). *The community of those who have nothing in common.* Bloomington, IN: Indiana University Press.

Makau, J., & Marty, D. (2013). *Dialogue and deliberation.* Long Grove, IL: Waveland.

Moe, K. (2004, Summer). Change starts with your own story. *Yes! Magazine, 70,* 47–50.

Mouffe, C. (2000). *The democratic paradox.* New York, NY: Verso.

Nabatchi, T., & Leighninger, M. (2015). *Public participation for the 21st century.* Hoboken, NJ: Wiley.

Oakes, J., Lipton, M. Anderson, L., & Stillman, J. (2018). *Teaching to change the world* (5th ed.). New York, NY: Routledge.

Purpel, D. E. (1999*). Moral outrage in education.* New York, NY: Peter Lang.

Rozsa, L., Balingit, M., Wan, W., & Berman, M. (2018, February 15). "A horrific, horrific day": At least 17 killed in Florida school shooting. *Washington Post.* Available from https://www.washingtonpost.com/news/education/wp/2018/02/14/school-shooting-reported-at-florida-high-school/?utm_term=.ed4C10792e86

Schradie, J. (2018, February 5). Moral Monday is more than a hashtag: The strong ties of social movement emergence in the digital era. *Social Media, Activism and Organizations,* 1–13. doi:1O.1177/2056305117750719

Swartz, O., Campbell, K., & Pestana, C. (2009). *Neo-pragmatism, communication, and the culture of creative democracy.* New York, NY: Peter Lang.

Williams, M. (2009). Feminism, first-wave. In G. Misioroglu (Ed.), *American countercultures: An encyclopedia of nonconformists, alternative lifestyles, and radical ideas in U.S. history* (Vol. 1) (pp. 254–256). Armonk, NY: Sharpe Reference.

Zinn, H. (2015). A *people's history of the United States.* New York, NY: Harper Perennial.

Social Media and Communication Ethics

Do you remember the first time you posted something on a social media platform? Was your first social media platform Facebook? Instagram? Do you remember the first time someone posted something embarrassing about you and tagged you in the post? Since at least 2004, friends and family have been able to embarrass each other in highly public ways. For instance, consider an article written by Sonia Bokhari, who was 13 when she "saw the pictures that [her mom] had been posting on Facebook for years. [She] felt utterly embarrassed, and deeply betrayed. There, for anyone to see on her public Facebook account, were all of the embarrassing moments from [her] childhood" (Bokhari, 2019, para. 4 and 5).

Over the past 10 to 20 years, traditional distinctions between mass communication ethics (or media ethics) and ethics in human communication have lost much of their value. With the wide use of social networks, internet-capable cell phones, and other digital technologies, mass communication and interpersonal communication have become intertwined in ways that were not imagined at the dawn of the digital age. World-changing events, such as the Arab Spring, have been linked to the strength and personal connections of mediated social networks, along with traditional media (Khondker, 2011; Wiest & Eltantawy, 2012). Tragedies like the suicide of a "16-year-old from... Tennessee" who took "his own life...after two classmates publicized screenshots of explicit text conversations he had with another young man" (Willingham, 2019, para. 1). The student "shot and killed himself after friends posted chats on Snapchat and Instagram that outed the teen as bisexual" (para. 2). In years past, rumors could have been spread, but it would not have been possible to share a private written conversation to a broad audience.

Communication ethics has traditionally been broken down into two general areas with only a small area of overlap: media ethics and ethics in human communication. Typically, scholars and students of media ethics or mass communication ethics have focused on mediated, one-way communication. They might discuss ethical issues related to such things as broadcast or print journalism, television or film, advertising, public relations, or the effects of media on audiences. In these contexts, communication is often described as a message sent to a larger audience through a medium with little or no instant feedback from the receiver.

Ethics in human communication, on the other hand, has largely focused on communication in a variety of relationships where the responses are more simultaneous or focused on the ethical aspects of the message. Scholars in these situations often assume face-to-face communication, or communication within small groups and organizations, which was assumed to be synchronous and two-way. Social media and digital technology allow mass communication and human communication to intermingle. While you can share a message broadly on a social media platform, you are often sharing that message with people with whom you have a relationship, and the feedback can be immediate and tailored to the other person. Communication that most people would assume would be private (text messages, individual messages within social media platforms) can be forwarded to others or screen-shotted and shared widely on social media platforms. In the past, where rumors might have spread in a small, local area, the same information can be shared over and over to an ever-widening audience.

Historically, scholars studying both media ethics and ethics in human communication have been concerned with the same types of issues, including privacy, confidentiality, lying, secrets, stereotyping, civility, accuracy, and truth. To illustrate this point, let's consider the issue of privacy, which is important in both media ethics and interpersonal communication ethics.

Concerns about privacy in the mass media often focus on the extent to which the personal lives of politicians and celebrities should be revealed. For instance, Dax Shepherd and Kristen Bell led a campaign, called the *No Kids Policy* to shield the children of celebrities from the tabloids and paparazzi (Goodman, 2014). This came after many experiences where celebrities had to fight for their children's privacy. While the policy has protected many celebrity children, some children of superstars still face intense scrutiny. In 2019, a family photograph of Beyoncé's young children was leaked to the celebrity press (Davis, 2019). Similarly, the press has often debated whether extramarital affairs of politicians should be revealed to the public; until the Gary Hart scandal of the late 1980s, the press typically did not disclose when a male politician had a mistress (Bai, 2014). When examining privacy from an interpersonal communication perspective, the biggest concern is often gossip that was spread among a group of friends or acquaintances. While the issue for an individual might have been the same as it was for a person in the public eye, an extramarital affair, individuals generally did not have to worry about private information going beyond their personal networks. In today's networked world, privacy is difficult to maintain. Cell phones with cameras and internet access mean that an embarrassing moment, moral lapse, or faux pas can instantly be made available for others beyond those present to see and comment on.

There are many other ethical issues that are related to using social media, including how social media and technology use may positively or negatively affect your relationships with the people you are closest to, how the design of social media platforms might differ depending on the ethical perspective that underlies it, how the internet service provider you choose might bias the information you get, or how using different values would change the terms of service of social media platforms. You might also be concerned with cyberbullying, trolling, and stalking. Many of these are ethical issues because the actions taken are not illegal, but cause harm to others through intentional communication.

Chapter Activities

Many of us use social media with little thought about whether it is ethical. Your parents probably posted pictures of your childhood on Facebook and Instagram. How old were you when you started to object? Why did it bother you? What do you think when your friends post pictures or videos of you? In all of these cases, you probably felt like your privacy was violated. The activities in this section will help you examine privacy, dialogic ethics, how different ethical perspectives might change the design of social media platforms; how terms of service may infringe on your rights; and how internet services are provided.

Privacy: What is it?

In the first activity, you will define what privacy is and discuss whether you value it. People in their teens and twenties often believe that they have no privacy because of how they use their smart phones, but often object to other people posting pictures or videos of them (Bokhari, 2019). As you further think about privacy, you might start to worry about smart apartments, where management might know when you leave and return to your apartment (Wood, 2019), without your consent. In the activity about privacy, you will consider an example of what many consider a privacy violation because of technology and you will define privacy and determine its importance in your life.

Dialogic Ethics and Social Media

How much time do you spend online each day? If you have your phone in front of you as you read this, check your daily time online using the Screen Time feature on an iPhone (go to *Settings–Screen Time*) or the Device Care feature on an Android (go to *Settings–Device Care*). Do you think that your phone ever interferes with your relationships with your family and friends? According to researchers, smart phone use can affect how connected parents feel to their children (Kushlev & Dun, 2019) and how connected people feel to their friends and partners (Chotpitayasunondh & Douglas, 2018; Vogels & Anderson, 2020). One way to see how much your relationships are affected by your smartphone is by participating in this activity, where you spend 24 hours limiting your device usage and focusing on using a dialogic ethics approach to connecting with your acquaintances, classmates, friends, and family members. As a reminder, a dialogic approach to communication ethics is where you aim to be present for the other, acting as an empathetic listener and partner in conversations.

What Do You Give Up to Keep Up with Your Friends?

How many social media apps do you have on your phone? When you signed up for these apps, how carefully did you read the terms of service (TOS)? Are the terms of service consistent with your values? When we think about values, we are thinking about important ideas like truth, justice, freedom, care, integrity, and honor (Tompkins, 2019). Are the terms of service consistent with the ethical perspectives you've been learning about? This activity gives you the opportunity to examine all of these questions and create terms of service for a hypothetical social media app.

Designing a Social Media Platform Based on Ethical Perspectives

Imagine you could design a social media platform based on an ethical perspective of your choice. How would it differ from what is currently available? Some research shows a relationship between grandiose narcissism and frequent social media use (McCain & Campbell, 2018). Furthermore, users of current platforms often face challenges related to cyberbullying, trolling, and stalkers (Swenson-Lepper & Kerby, 2019). Are there ways you could design a social media platform that might prevent some of these problems? How would social media platforms be different if you used a deontological approach, where you act in the way that is morally correct, regardless of the consequences to others? How about if you used situational ethics, where you act on what is most loving for the other person? What if you designed a platform based on utilitarian ethics, where you consider what is the greatest good for the greatest number of people? As you can see, these are difficult questions; answering them might change how you view the social media apps you currently use.

No More Net Neutrality

In this activity, you are asked to consider what happens when net neutrality regulations are suspended. Net neutrality is the idea that, regardless of the website or streaming service, your internet service provider (ISP) doesn't charge a premium so that those services can have access to you, the ISP's customer. Of the issues raised in this section, this one has the widest societal implications. For instance, if your ISP is Comcast (Xfinity), they own NBCUniversal (Johnston, 2020), which means they might charge Netflix, CBS All Access, or Disney+ additional fees to have higher speeds on their network. Basically, if the services you pay for don't pay a premium to your ISP, you may face really slow download speeds. This hampers smaller apps and websites, who might not be able to afford the fees charged by the ISPs. If you could influence Congress to change federal regulations about net neutrality, would you? What ethical perspective would you base the changes on?

© Michael Candelori/Shutterstock.com

References

Bai, M. (2014, September 18). How Gary Hart's downfall forever changed American politics. *The New York Times Magazine.* https://www.nytimes.com/2014/09/21/magazine/how-gary-harts-downfall-forever-changed-american-politics.html

Bokhari, S. (2019, March 18). I'm 14, and I quit social media after discovering what was posted about me. *Fast Company.* https://www.fastcompany.com/90315706/kids-parents-social-media-sharing

Chotpitayasunondh, V., & Douglas, K. M. (2018). The effects of 'phubbing' on social interaction. *Journal of Applied Social Psychology, 48*(6), 304–316. https://doi.org/10.1111/jasp.12506

Davis, A. (2019, April 4). A photo of Beyoncé's children was leaked on Instagram—and that's not okay. *O: Oprah Magazine.* https://www.oprahmag.com/entertainment/a27042965/beyonce-leaked-private-photos-kids/

Goodman, J. (2014, June 10). Kristen Bell says No Kids Policy has already changed lives. *Huffpost.* https://www.huffpost.com/entry/kristen-bell-no-kids-policy-interview_n_5478488

Johnston, M. (2020). 5 companies owned by comcast: Broadband, media and entertainment, film, broadcast and telecommunications. Investopedia. https://www.investopedia.com/articles/markets/101215/top-4-companies-owned-comcast.asp

Khondker, H. H. (2011). The role of new media in the Arab Spring. *Globalizations, 8*(5), 675–679. https://doi.org/10.1080/14747731.2011.621287

Kushlev, K., & Dun, E. W. (2019). Smartphones distract parents from cultivating feelings of connection when spending time with their children. *Journal of Social & Personal Relationships, 36*(6), 1619–1639. https://doi.org/10.1177/0265407518769387

McCain, J. L., & Campbell, W. K. (2018). Narcissism and social media use: A meta-analytic review. *Psychology of Popular Media Culture, 7*(3), 308–327. https://doi.org/10.1037/ppm0000137

Swenson-Lepper, T., & Kerby, A. (2019). Cyberbullies, trolls, and stalkers: Students' perceptions of ethical issues in social media, *Journal of Media Ethics, 34*(2), 102–113. https://doi.org/10.1080/23736992.2019.1599721

Tompkins, P. (2019). *Practicing communication ethics: Development discernment, and decision making* (2nd ed.). Routledge.

Vogels, E. A., & Anderson, M. (2020, May 8). Dating and relationships in the digital age. Pew Research Center: Internet and Technology. https://www.pewresearch.org/internet/2020/05/08/dating-and-relationships-in-the-digital-age/

Wiest, J. B., & Eltantawy, N. (2012). Social media use among UAE college students one year after the Arab Spring. *Journal of Arab & Muslim Media Research, 5*(3), 209–226.

Willingham, A. J. (2019, September 30). The family of a teen who died by suicide after being outed by cyberbullies is demanding justice. *CNN.* https://www.cnn.com/2019/09/30/us/channing-smith-suicide-cyberbullying-tennessee-trnd/index.html

Wood, M. (2019, March 5). Do renters have the right to reject smart home technology? Marketplace. https://www.marketplace.org/2019/03/05/tech/do-renters-have-the-right-to-dumb-apartments/

Additional Resources

[1]boyd, d. (2014). *It's complicated: The social lives of networked teens.* Yale University Press.

*[2]Bowles, N. (2018, October 26). The digital gap between rich and poor kids is not what we expected. *The New York Times.* https://www.nytimes.com/2018/10/26/style/digital-divide-screens-schools.html

Buckels, E. E., Trapnell, P. D., & Paulhus, D. L. (2014). Trolls just want to have fun. *Personality and Individual Differences, 67,* 97–102. https://doi.org/10.1016/j.paid.2014.01.016

---

[1] The author prefers that her first and last name not be capitalized.

[2] All references marked with an asterisk (*) are newspaper articles that might provide context for students.

Drouin, M., O'Connor, K. W., Schmidt, G. B., & Miller, D. A. (2015). Facebook fired: Legal perspectives and young adults' opinions on the use of social media in hiring and firing decisions. *Computers in Human Behavior, 46*, 123–128. https://doi.org/10.1016/j.chb.2015.01.011

*Frenkel, S., Isaac, M., & Conger, K. (2018). On Instagram, 11,696 examples of how hate thrives on social media. *The New York Times.* https://www.nytimes.com/2018/10/29/technology/hate-on-social-media.html

German, K., & Drushel, B. (Eds.). (2011). *The ethics of emerging media.* Continuum.

*Lohr, St. (2018, December 4). Digital divide is wider than we think, study says. *The New York Times.* https://www.nytimes.com/2018/12/04/technology/digital-divide-us-fcc-microsoft.html

*Markkula Center for Applied Ethics. (2013). Selfies. https://www.scu.edu/the-big-q/the-big-q-blog/selfies.html

Phillips, W. (2015). *This is why we can't have nice things: Mapping the relationship between online trolling and mainstream culture* (Reprint edition). Boston, MA: The MIT Press.

*Popescu, A. (2019, January 22). Why people ghost—and how to get over it. *The New York Times.*

**[3]Schulman, M. (2011). Facebook gossip or cyberbullying? Markkula Center for Applied Ethics. Santa Clara University. https://www.scu.edu/the-big-q/the-big-q-blog/facebook-gossip-or-cyberbullying.html

**Schulman, M. (2011). Sexting. Markkula Center for Applied Ethics. Santa Clara University. https://www.scu.edu/the-big-q/the-big-q-blog/sexting.html

Shirky, C. (2009). How social media can make history [video]. Ted. https://www.ted.com/talks/clay_shirky_how_social_media_can_make_history?referrer=playlist-the_power_of_social_media#t-8809

**Varma, A. (2019, September 24). Ethical storytelling on social media. Markkula Center for Applied Ethics. Santa Clara University. https://www.scu.edu/ethics/ethical-dilemmas-in-the-social-sector/ethical-storytelling-on-social-media/

**Vyas, A. (2013). Browsing or cyberstalking? Markkula Center for Applied Ethics. Santa Clara University. https://www.scu.edu/the-big-q/the-big-q-blog/browsing-or-cyberstalking.html

**Wilson, C. (2013). Can you keep a secret? Markkula Center for Applied Ethics. Santa Clara University. https://www.scu.edu/the-big-q/the-big-q-blog/can-you-keep-a-secret.html

**Wilson, C. (2013). Insta-interruption. Markkula Center for Applied Ethics. Santa Clara University. https://www.scu.edu/the-big-q/the-big-q-blog/insta-interruption.html

Wong, P. (2013). Confucian social media: An oxymoron? *Dao, 12*, 283–296.

---

[3] All references marked with ** are case studies that might be useful in class.

Privacy

What Is It?

Imagine this scenario: you've just graduated from college and you are moving to a different city to take a job. Your new job pays you well enough that you can rent a decent apartment. Your leasing agent takes you to several buildings, and for many of the buildings, she points out that all of the properties are *smart apartments*. You are familiar with smart devices like Alexa and Google Home, but you're not familiar with smart apartments, so you decide to do a little research and you come across this article, which is a transcript of a radio broadcast from Marketplace, a show on National Public Radio about personal finance.

> *Smart homes full of connected devices aren't just for those who own their houses. And if you're a renter, you might get a smart apartment whether you want one or not. In January 2019, security researcher and blogger Lesley Carhart got a letter from her landlord saying their building was getting internet-connected door locks. Her response was, "No, thank you." Host Molly Wood talked with Carhart about the big business of smart apartments. The following is an edited transcript of their conversation.*

> *Molly Wood: What are the pros of smart apartments?*

> *Lesley Carhart: There are a lot of good reasons for implementing this technology. First of all, it makes it easier for rental properties to manage and maintain the units, especially when they're unoccupied. They can do things like monitor for water leaks. They can also make an added convenience for their users, which is a good sell for potential residents. You can change your temperature from your phone. You can grant access to people when you're not home and know who's accessing your apartment when. There are a lot of benefits in terms of convenience and also the ability for apartment management companies to require less staff to do things like show apartments.*

> *Wood: What are the cons, ranging from physical security to privacy?*

> *Carhart: I often tell people that, in terms of security, things can be quick, cheap, secure, but not all three at once. In this case, the industry is asking for this to be implemented quickly and cheaply. Consumers really need to be asking for security here for multiple reasons. First of all, you're sending a tremendous amount of data about the way that you live, who's home, when you're home, when you go to work. You're sending that out over the internet to multiple parties. You would ostensibly want to send that securely. Also, the lock, of course, is granting access to your apartment. You want to be certain that nobody malicious can grant access to your apartment in a way that, unlike breaking into a window or breaking a lock off a door, is not really easily detectable (Wood, 2019, para. 1-5).*

Loss of privacy is a significant ethical issue, especially as we use more free online apps that require information from us so that we can access the tool (Rainie & Duggan, 2016). Social media platforms mine data from our profiles, as do search engines and shopping sites. Before we give up our privacy, it is important for us to understand the value of personal privacy and how easily it is lost. Privacy is an

© Rawpixel.com

often-discussed issue in media and journalism ethics, but is more complicated in the age of social media, the internet, and online tools. For instance, when you use a mapping tool, you provide information about where you physically are located and plan to go. With many social media apps, you can decide what information you share with others: friends, acquaintances, or strangers. New technology (Wood, 2019) as mentioned in the introduction, allows landlords to know when you leave and enter your apartment. Does this make you feel safe or feel like Big Brother is watching your every move?

In this activity you will increase your *knowledge* by considering:

- What is privacy? How is it defined?

- Does the definition of privacy change, depending on the context? (online or face-to-face)

- Does the definition change depending on the people with whom you are communicating?

In this activity, you will reflect on your own *values* by inquiring about:

- Why is privacy important to us?

- What are we trying to protect and how is that ethical?

- Is privacy more important to you in some situations?

- Are you concerned about privacy when it comes to financial or personal information?

Defining Privacy

Step One

Define privacy. As you create your definition, Google the term "privacy" and develop a definition in your own words that is between 50 and 100 words long. Write it below, on your class discussion board, or on a notecard, as directed by your instructor.

My definition of privacy:

Number of words: _____

Step Two

Online Class: Follow your instructor's directions for the number of posts you should comment on.
In Person Class: After you create your definition of privacy, everyone's definition of privacy will be collected, mixed up, and all definitions will be given to groups assigned by your instructor. Each group should, based on the definitions in front of them, come up with one new definition that you can all agree on. You should write this definition on your group's white board or other shared space as noted by your instructor.

Step Three

Online Class: On your class discussion board, note your favorite definition and explain why it is your favorite.
In Person Class: Everyone in the class will vote on the definition they think is best. Your group cannot vote for your own definition.

Discussion Questions

Once the top definition is determined, discuss the following:

1. Why was the top definition the best?

2. What characteristics made it better than others?

3. Does your definition of privacy change, depending on the context (online or face-to-face)? Does the definition change depending on the people with whom you are communicating?

4. Is privacy more important to you in some situations? Are you concerned about privacy when it comes to financial or personal information?

5. Are there times when privacy might be harmful? For instance, companies often claim that salary information is private, but this often hurts women and minorities because they can't compare their salary to the salary of their peers (Wong, 2019).

References

Rainie, L., & Duggan, M. (2016, January 14). Privacy and information sharing. Pew Research Center: Internet, Science & Tech. https://www.pewinternet.org/2016/01/14/privacy-and-information-sharing/

Wong, K. (2019, January 20). Want to close the pay gap? Pay transparency will help. *The New York Times.* https://www.nytimes.com/2019/01/20/smarter-living/pay-wage-gap-salary-secrecy-transparency.html

Wood, M. (2019, March 5). Do renters have the right to reject smart home technology? Marketplace. https://www.marketplace.org/2019/03/05/tech/do-renters-have-the-right-to-dumb-apartments/

Additional Resources

Carman, A. (2019, July 17). FaceApp is back and so are privacy concerns: Think before you upload. *The Verge.* https://www.theverge.com/2019/7/17/20697771/faceapp-privacy-concerns-ios-android-old-age-filter-russia

Rainie, L., & Anderson, J. (2014, December 18). The future of privacy. Pew Research Center: Internet, Science & Tech. http://www.pewinternet.org/2014/12/18/future-of-privacy/

Rainie, L., & Madden, M. (2015, March 16). American's privacy strategies post-Snowden. Pew Research Center: Internet, Science & Tech. http://www.pewinternet.org/2015/03/16/Americans-Privacy-Strategies-Post-Snowden/

Scott, A. (Host). (2021, May 17). Smart devices are listening to more than our words [Audio podcast episode]. In *Marketplace Tech.* Stephanie Hughes. https://www.marketplace.org/shows/marketplace-tech/smart-devices-could-listen-emotions-physical-state/?fbclid=IwAR0pCZJ1uNs5JK-jVkzoawrNZerh-XNvb5ClAi1v_cl3VO9F7gcls8Su0Qs8

What Americans think about privacy. (2014, November 12). Pew Research Center: Internet, Science & Tech. http://www.pewinternet.org/2014/11/12/what-americans-think-about-privacy/

Dialogic Ethics and Social Media

Does this sound like you? You are walking to class across campus, so you decide to check your texts and social media apps. Later that day in the dining hall, one of your friends tells you that she said "hi" to you when she met you on the sidewalk, but you were too engrossed in your phone to notice her. Or, what about this example? You and your friends go out for dinner at your favorite restaurant, only to have everyone stare at their phones for the entire meal (Castrodale, 2018). Does this leave you feeling disconnected from your family and friends? What if there were ways to learn how to better connect with your friends and family? This activity will help you more carefully consider how and when you are going to use technology mindfully.

In this activity, you will increase your *knowledge* by considering:

- What is genuine dialogue?

- What does it mean to be fully present?

- What is dialogic ethics from the perspective of Martin Buber?

In this activity, you will learn *skills* by asking yourself:

- How can I be a better listener and relational partner in a wide variety of relational contexts?

- What behaviors do I need to change to have more dialogic communication with significant relational partners?

In this activity, you will reflect on your own *values* by:

- Asking yourself whether it is important for you and your relationships to be more present with your friends, in your classes, and in your workplace. Would putting away your device show that you value your relationship? Why or why not?

- Are there circumstances where other values might be greater than the value of the relationship you are currently involved in, where you might choose to keep interacting with your phone? In what situations would that occur?

- What obstacles to genuine dialogue need to be removed or guarded against?

In this activity, you could take *action* by:

- Learning how much time you spend on your phone. What do your usage statistics tell you about how much you use your phone?

- Turning off or putting away your devices when you are involved in conversation with others. How would taking this action make you feel? How hard would it be?

The Activity

1. Spend 24 hours being fully present and use a dialogic perspective with your friends, peers, and school and work colleagues (do your best!).

2. What does this mean?
   - Pick a class day and be "fully present" in your classes by focusing only on the course material and discussions surrounding the material.
   - Put away all media, except that which is needed for class.
   - Engage with your professors and colleagues—stay focused, listen to what they are saying, and ask questions.

3. Don't interrupt conversations to check texts, social media, or email. Wait until your current conversation is over to communicate with others not involved in the current situation.

4. Pay attention to how much time you spend using your phone, laptop, and iPad. Do they interfere with your relationships? Your ability to let your mind wander?

Discussion Questions

1. What did it mean to you to be fully present in a class?

2. How did being "present" change the way you interacted with your classmates and your professor?

3. How did the size of the class affect your ability to be fully "present"?

4. Upon reflection over the last few days, what most surprised you about doing this activity? Why did it surprise you? What did you learn about yourself? Others? What did you learn about dialogic ethics?

5. How hard was it to be fully "present"? Why? What did you learn about your listening skills?

6. Did participating in this challenge affect the way you perceive the use of media in classes? How? Do you perceive the use of media more positively or negatively? What guidelines would you give to other college students about how to ethically and effectively use media while they're in class?

Reference

Castrodale, J. (2018, February 28). Study confirms that you're making everyone miserable by checking your phone at dinner. *Vice*. https://www.vice.com/en_us/article/evmky4/study-confirms-that-youre-making-everyone-miserable-by-checking-your-phone-at-dinner

Additional Resources

Arnett, R. C., Arneson, P., & Bell, L. M. (2006). Communication ethics: The dialogic turn. *The Review of Communication*, 6(1&2), 62–92.

Buber, M. (1970). *I and thou*. Charles Scribner Sons. http://buber.de/en/i_thou

Caren, A. (2014). Redefining what it means to talk in the age of smartphones. All Tech Considered: Tech, Culture and Connection. https://www.npr.org/sections/alltechconsidered/2014/06/22/323568848/redefining-what-it-means-to-talk-in-the-age-of-smartphones

Hampton, K., Rainie, L., Lu, W., Dwyer, M., Shin, I., & Purcell, K. (2014, August 26). Social media and the 'spiral of silence.' Pew Research Center: Internet & Technology. https://www.pewinternet.org/2014/08/26/social-media-and-the-spiral-of-silence/

What Do You Give Up to Keep Up with Your Friends?

Giving Up Your Rights: Terms of Service

How many social media apps do you have on your phone? How many times have you read the terms of service for those apps? Instead of reading the terms of service, have you simply clicked *Accept*? I know I have. Unfortunately, when you agree to terms of service, you often give up rights to your own materials and the privacy of your data. For instance, spread throughout TikTok's lengthy Terms of Service, you give the app permission to change, use, and own your image and videos that you post to their site. In the "User-Generated Content" section, TikTok indicates that when you sign your agreement, you grant them "unconditional, irrevocable. . ." permission to use, change or publish your work in any way that they'd like (section Content #9, para. 6). In the section labeled, "TikTok Content," you give the app permission to use your work to generate revenue for TikTok—and you give up the right to any of that income (section Content, #7, para 2). Check it out for yourself at https://www. tiktok.com/legal/terms-of-use?lang=en! Doesn't that surprise you? Did you know that when you posted to TikTok (and other social media apps), that you were giving the app and its owners the freedom to publish your face and work without your permission?

In this activity, you will increase your *knowledge* by considering:

- What are the terms of services for the apps you use most often?

- Were you surprised by the terms of service? Why or why not? What was most surprising (if anything) about the terms of service of the apps you use?

In this activity, you will learn *skills* by investigating:

- How to create your own terms of service.

- What would you include that is different from current apps?

In this activity, you will reflect on your own *values* by inquiring:

- What values would you want your terms of service to reflect? Why?

- How would ethical perspectives affect your terms of service?

The Activity

1. Think about terms of service for a social media platform.

   a. You can find the Terms of Service for Snapchat at https://www.snap.com/en-US/terms/

   b. The Terms of Service for Instagram at https://help.instagram.com/581066165581870 and Instagram's community guidelines here: https://help.instagram.com/477434105621119

   c. TikTok's can be found here: https://www.tiktok.com/legal/terms-of-use

2. Consider the terms of service for the platform(s) you have examined. What did the terms of service tell you about how the platform will use your information? What rights do you have to your information, pictures, or videos when you are using the app?

3. Create new terms of service for the user community based on two of the following perspectives. Please pick perspectives that challenge you (your instructor might also assign you a perspective that's not on this list).

   a. *Virtue ethics.* Virtue ethics focuses on being a person of good character.

   b. *Consequentialist ethics.* Utilitarian ethics focuses on the greatest good for the greatest number.

   c. *Duty ethics.* When using a deontological perspective, you would always choose to act in the most ethical manner, regardless of the consequences. For instance, you would never lie, even to save a life.

   d. *Dialogic ethics.* In dialogic ethics, communicators must be fully present with each other, and not regard the other as an object to be used.

   e. *Feminist ethics.* This perspective focuses on expressing care and minimizing harm.

   You should have at least seven items for each term of service. The most common issues discussed in terms of service are related to (1) the corporation's rights to your content and personal information, (2) impersonation, (3) acting unlawfully, (4) violating others' rights, (5) appropriateness of postings, etc. Should that be the case? Are other values, specifically user rights, as or more important?

Ethical Perspective 1: _____	Ethical Perspective 2: _____
1.	1.
2.	2.
3.	3.
4.	4.
5.	5.
6.	6.
7.	7.

Discussion Questions

1. What surprised you about the terms of service for your favorite social media apps? Do the terms of service you reviewed affect your willingness to use social media or the way you will use social media in the future? Why or why not?

2. How does creating terms of services based on an ethical perspective affect your views of the current social media platforms you use?

3. If you oversaw writing terms of service, would you want to make them more readable for average people signing up for the apps? Why or why not? If you think the terms of service are overly complicated, what would you specifically do as a writer to simplify them? What writing skills would you need?

4. Would you prefer to use a social media platform based on one of the ethical perspectives you looked at? Why or why not? Does one of the options you've created match your values more?

5. Have you ever considered deleting an app because of their terms of service? Why or why not?

Reference

TikTok (2019, February). Terms of Service. https://www.tiktok.com/legal/terms-of-use?lang=en

Additional Resources

This activity works particularly well with non-Western perspectives on communication ethics. The following resources are particularly readable for students.

Berzin, A. (2011). Applying Buddhist principles for the age of social media: Unedited transcript. Berzin Archives. http://www.berzinarchives.com/web/en/archives/approaching_buddhism/world_today/appl_bst_principles_age_soc_media/transcript.html

Ishii, S. (2009). Conceptualising Asian communication ethics: A Buddhist perspective. *Journal of Multicultural Discourses, 4*(1), 49–60. Double checking Conceptualizing

Mowlana, H. (2007). Theoretical perspectives on Islam and communication. *China Media Research, 3*(4), 23–33.

Wong, P. (2013). Confucian social media: An oxymoron? *Dao, 12*, 283–296.

Designing a Social Media Platform Based on Ethical Perspectives

How many social media platforms do you use daily? Do you use Twitter? Instagram? TikTok? Snapchat? How about Facebook (Perrin & Anderson, 2019)? More than likely, you use TikTok a lot, and you only use Facebook to keep in touch with older family members. TikTok use has grown rapidly with teens and college-aged people (Mohsin, 2020). These social media apps are based on individualist assumptions about communication and human behavior. But, what if we based the creation of a social media app on an ethical or philosophical perspective? How would that change how an app works? How would it change how you use an app or what you post? How would it change who you interact with, how often, and the types of interactions you have?

This activity is a thought experiment where you will work either individually or with a group to design social media apps based on different ethical perspectives. You might be surprised at how different the apps are, depending on the perspectives you use.

In this activity, you will increase your *knowledge* by considering:

- How are social media apps designed?

- How the icon/symbol for a social media platform reflects its values.

- How would the use of different ethical perspectives lead to social media platforms with different designs?

- How key terms (anonymity, privacy, friendship circles, multiple audiences, synchronicity vs. asynchronicity, membership level, and role responsibility) are related to social media platforms.

In this activity, you will reflect on your own *values* by inquiring:

- How would different ethical values affect the design of social media platforms?

- What ethical values are more important when designing a social media platform?

- How would incorporating different values shape how you communicate with others?

In this activity, you will take action by:

- Imagining how your app would work in real life. What steps would you take to make it real?

- What types of people do you think would be interested in your app?

The Activity

Based on the ethical perspectives you or your group have been assigned, design a social media platform that lives up to the principles of your ethical perspective. Your instructor will tell you the three perspectives you or your group should look at.

- Virtue ethics

- Consequentialist ethics

- Duty ethics
- Dialogic ethics
- Feminist ethics

NOTE: Additional ethical perspectives can be chosen based on professor's preference or goals.

1. As you are designing your social media platform, think about how each ethical perspective would deal with the following issues and fill them in on the table on the next page:

   a. Anonymity: no one knows who you are

   b. Privacy: the ability to keep information you want to protect away from others

   c. Friendship circles (i.e., friends, followers, etc.): in many social media platforms you can choose who sees which posts, depending on their status as your follower

   d. Multiple audiences: some known, some unknown

   e. Asynchronicity versus synchronicity: asynchronicity in a platform is when a message is posted and viewed at a different time; synchronicity is when communication is happening simultaneously

   f. Membership level: would you join as an individual, as a family, a friend group, or something else? (Wong, 2013)

   g. Role responsibility: is the role you take on the social media platform a family role, social role, or organizational role? (Wong, 2013)

   h. Contextual awareness: the ability to know who might view or who has viewed your social media posts (Wong, 2013)

Term (see definitions above):	Perspective 1	Perspective 2	Perspective 3
Anonymity			
Privacy			
Friendship Circles			
Known and Unknown Audiences			
A-synchronicity vs. Synchronicity			
Membership Level			
Role Responsibility			
Contextual Awareness			

2. What would you call your social media network for each ethical perspective? Why? How does it relate to the ethical perspective? You should develop the name after you've thoroughly discussed the different perspectives so that your name best describes your new platform. Draw a sketch of your apps' logos.

App 1:

App 2:

App 3:

3. How do you imagine that interactions would differ on the social media platforms you've envisioned? Why?

4. After you've looked at all three perspectives, choose two social media platforms for you or your group to present to the class in a brief impromptu presentation. You should discuss (a) the names you gave your platforms and why, (b) the basic issues outlined in point one for each platform, and (c) how you envision interactions would differ depending on the platform and why they would differ.

5. Make sure that you come up with an introduction and conclusion; your introduction should have an attention getter and preview at the very least. Your conclusion should have a summary and a clincher.

Discussion Questions

1. How would social media platforms differ if they were based on different ethical perspectives? Are these differences significant?

2. Would you prefer that social media platforms were based on one of these ethical perspectives? Why or why not?

3. Do you see any ethical design features on any of the existing large social media platforms? (i.e., Twitter, TikTok, Facebook, Instagram, Snapchat, etc.), If so, what specific features? Do you think said features align with any of the ethical approaches to ethics?

4. Do you think that one of the social media platforms you created would actually work? Why or why not?

5. What steps could you take if you wanted to develop this app for use?

References

Mohsin, M. (2020, May 22). 10 TikTok statistics that you need to know in 2020. Oberlo. Retrieved on https://www.oberlo.com/blog/tiktok-statistics

Neher, W. W., & Sandin, P. J. (2017). *Communicating ethically: Character, duties, consequences, and relationships* (2nd ed.). New York: Routledge.

Perrin, A., & Anderson, M. (2019, April 10). Share of U.S. adults using social media, including Facebook, is mostly unchanged since 2018. Pew Research Center. Retrieved on https://www.pewresearch.org/fact-tank/2019/04/10/share-of-u-s-adults-using-social-media-including-facebook-is-mostly-unchanged-since-2018/

Additional Resource

The following article is an excellent introduction to a non-Western perspective on social media use.

Wong, P. (2013). Confucian social media: An oxymoron? *Dao, 12*(3), 283–296. Retrieved on https://doi.org/10.1007/s11712-013-9329-y

No More Net Neutrality?

For a great introduction to Net Neutrality, watch the first two videos by John Oliver, or, if you want to avoid profanity, watch the third one on the list:

1. Net neutrality: https://youtu.be/fpbOEoRrHyU (Oliver, 2014)

2. Net Neutrality II: https://youtu.be/92vuuZt7wak (Oliver, 2017)

3. Net Neutrality Is Dead: https://youtu.be/hIULYHz6BWA (from The Verge)

In sum, Net Neutrality regulations state that internet service providers (ISPs) cannot charge content providers (like Netflix, Hulu, or Disney1) a higher price so content providers can have faster service, which ensures that all content providers have the same streaming speed. The other side of this rule is that we, as consumers, will likely pay a slightly higher price for our internet service because streaming services aren't paying ISPs to provide more bandwidth and better download speeds. For instance, Comcast, which owns Xfinity, a very common residential ISP, also owns NBCUniversal (Johnston, 2020), making it likely that they would stream shows from NBC (like the new Peacock streaming service) to their consumers at a faster rate than they would stream Hulu, Netflix, Disney+ or other streaming services, unless those streaming services paid the ISP a fee.

In this activity, you will increase your *knowledge* by considering:

• What is net neutrality? How does it affect your own life?

• What ethical perspectives are relevant to this situation? How are they defined?

In this activity, you will learn *skills* by thinking about:

• How should you write a letter to your representative or senator to be effective?

• What is the best argument you can craft for addressing net neutrality?

In this activity, you will reflect on your own *values* by asking:

• What different ethical perspectives relate to net neutrality, and how do those perspectives reflect your own values?

• Is net neutrality important to society? Why or why not?

Putting what you learn into *action* means asking:

• Which representative or senator should you write to, in order to change federal regulations about net neutrality?

• What social action groups could you join that favor or oppose net neutrality?

• What would be the most ethical approach to the distribution of high-speed internet service?

Early in the Trump administration (Kang, 2017), net neutrality regulations were revoked, but the issue is currently being adjudicated in the courts.

For the first step, your instructor will assign you two ethical perspectives to consider and determine whether you are working on this project alone or in small groups.

- Virtue ethics

- Consequentialist ethics

- Duty ethics

- Dialogic ethics

- Feminist ethics

- Additional perspective _____

Ethical Perspective One: _____

Based on this ethical perspective, would you want Net Neutrality to be reinstated in federal law? Why or why not? Justify using the perspective.

Ethical Perspective Two: _____

Based on this ethical perspective, would you want Net Neutrality to be reinstated in federal law? Why or why not? Justify using the perspective.

Discussion Questions

1. First, if you were to lobby Congress for rules for ISPs, what information would be most important present to your elected leaders and why?

2. Second, how could you synthesize the two ethical perspectives you used to create a foundation for your recommendation to Congress? How would your recommendation change and/or stay the same?

3. Third, what would you tell Congress is the most ethical legislation they could pass? Why would it be the most ethical and most beneficial? On what ethical perspective(s) (grounds) do you base this?

4. What would you specifically write in your letter or email to your senator or representative that would be persuasive? To whom would you address this letter/or email? Will you send it?

References

Johnston, M. (2020, May 15). 5 companies owned by Comcast. Investopedia. https://www. investopedia.com/articles/markets/101215/top-4-companies-owned-comcast.asp

Kang, C. (2017, December 14). F.C.C. repeals net neutrality rules. *The New York Times*. https://www. nytimes.com/2017/12/14/technology/net-neutrality-repeal-vote.html

Net neutrality is dead, now what? (2018, June 11). The Verge. https://youtu.be/hIULYHz6BWA

Oliver, J. (2014, June 1). Net neutrality. Last Week Tonight with John Oliver. HBO. [Video]. https:// youtu.be/fpbOEoRrHyU

Oliver, J. (2017, May 7). Neutrality II. Last Week Tonight with John Oliver. HBO. [Video]. https:// youtu.be/92vuuZt7wak

Additional Resources

Cohan, P. S. (2015, March 2). What does net neutrality mean for consumers? *Telegram & Gazette*, A10.

Kang, C. (2019, February 1). Net neutrality repeal at stake in as key court case starts. *The New York Times*. https://www.nytimes.com/2019/02/01/technology/net-neutrality-repeal-case.html

Molla, R. (2017, June 20). More than 60 million urban Americans don't have access to or can't afford broadband internet. *Vox*. https://www.vox.com/2017/6/20/15839626/disparity-between-urban-rural-internet-access-major-economies

Reese, N. (2018, February 5). FCC report concludes US internet speeds are 'Among worst in the developed world.' Broadbandnow. https://broadbandnow.com/report/2018-fcc-international-data-insights/

Shavin, N. (2014, July 2). Are Google and Amazon the next threat to Net Neutrality? *Forbes*. https:// www.forbes.com/sites/naomishavin/2014/07/02/are-google-and-amazon-the-next-threat-to-net-neutrality/#101b66f479c9

Smith, M. D. (2015, March 2/9). A civil-rights victory: Net neutrality is crucial to #BlackLivesMatter. *The Nation*, 4.

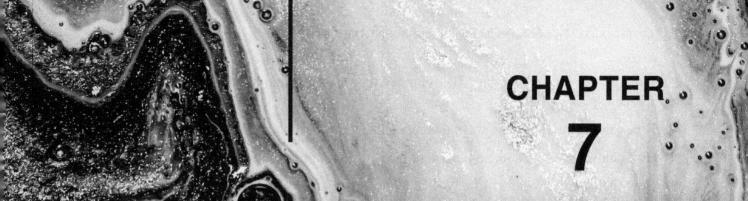

Putting Ethics into Your Everyday Practice

Here we are at the last chapter of the book, but of course it's only the beginning of your practice to communicate ethically in your life every day! This book and the activities were specifically designed to help you to begin that practice where you critically think and reflect on how ethics and communication intersect in your personal interactions and public life. Communication ethics assumes:

- Communicative acts are important, not trivial.

- Communication creates or constitutes our social world.

- Communication is reasoned, virtuous, habitual, and just.

- Through the lens of ethics, communication expresses the promise of pluralism and the requirement to exercise fairness, kindness, truthfulness, and respect toward another.

- Ethical choice points require communicative responses of some (ethical) kind.

- Communication not only expresses, but also enacts or enables ethical expression.

The centrality of communication ethics in your life cannot be overstated. Every day, no matter what you do, you will encounter opportunities to make choices that are better or worse. We hope by now you have honed your new *knowledge* to complement your *skills* and *values* in order to take the kind of *action* for which you can always be proud.

We have offered you a lot of questions to consider in this book to aid you in making decisions and working with others. As you might expect, we have even more questions for you to think about as you imagine your future. Communication ethics covers a lot of ground by asking:

- What should I say or do in any given situation? Speak, listen, wait, remain silent, advocate, resist, or something else?

- Do I understand the facts and different perspectives? What can I add to the conversation to deepen understanding for all?

- What are other people saying? To whom are they speaking and in what terms? For what ends are they speaking?

- How can I communicate in ways that recognize the contributions and needs of others?

- How can we speak to address persistent inequalities to promote positive social change?

- How shall we live together in ways that demonstrate respect for others?

- How can we communicate in ways that express care, justice, fairness, rules, truthfulness, and authenticity?

- Who will be impacted by the decisions I make, and in what ways?

- Who can speak, when, and in what forums, to whom, and with what influence?

- Who has access to speak and deliberate? Who confronts barriers to access and how can we mitigate those obstacles?

- What is the role of emotion in reasoned communication?

- What are the norms of ethical communication in specific contexts?

Continue asking questions of yourself and others! When you do, you inspire greater critical thinking that is essential for considering options that benefit you and others, while at the same time determining how best to respond to situations in any given moment and managing conflicts and dilemmas that inevitably come your way.

Bringing it all together, we know you will remember that communication ethics is value-laden. Even when your values are different than others, you now have tools to help you navigate conversational terrain. In that way, communication ethics posits a deep concern for the needs and legitimate expectations of others as well as your own. Your values and commitments, as well as others', are revealed in communication, reflecting varied cultural, societal, religious/spiritual, and familial values. As you might expect, we think words matter, a lot! So, what you say to express your convictions or perspective needs to be able to stand up to the questions posed by others.

Chapter Activities

We know there are a number of ways that you can clearly demonstrate how you bring together your understanding and practice of communication ethics. With that in mind, we offer a number of final activities in this chapter. Your instructor will guide you in choosing which activities are best for you to complete.

Wrapping it Up

This activity asks you to reflect on the most important things you've learned about communication ethics. Think about what stands out for you and why as you complete a worksheet first individually, then as a small group.

Crafting Your Ethical Voice

How will you use your ethical voice to advance a good life? This assignment requires that you offer a clear description of a situation you are likely to encounter in your future. Maybe you will be an active member of your community (maybe even a politician!), or perhaps you already have a future mission trip planned connected to your place of worship to provide service to others. It could be your plan to help manage disaster relief, start a new business, volunteer as a youth coach, or manage family finances for aging parents. You may not know exactly what lies in your future, but you probably have a sense of your future responsibilities. Your life will be put into the spotlight while writing this paper.

Your Ethical Credo: Putting Principles into Practice

The goal of this assignment is to write a paper that is different than most research papers you've probably written in the past. Here, you'll develop a personal statement on what you think people's rights and responsibilities are when communicating in the networked world. You'll talk about ethical perspectives and do additional scholarly research in a paper that features the nexus of theory and concrete practice.

Why Communication Ethics is an Important Course

With this assignment, you will prepare a presentation, using examples from your life to discuss how and why communication ethics is an important course for all students to take. You will combine personal stories and examples with a review of some ethical perspectives into a fully developed speech.

Wrapping It Up

What are the most important things you've learned about communication ethics? Was it a certain perspective, an ancient insight, or a new awareness? Think about the ideas, concepts, perspectives, and terms you've read about and the discussions and activities you completed. You might even review your completed activities as a way to remember all that you learned.

Just as valuable as identifying the most important things you learned is thinking about why those things were significant.

In this activity, you will increase your *knowledge* by considering:

- What category of communication ethics stands out as relevant to you?

- What concepts and perspectives did you learn that will guide your future thinking?

In this activity, you will learn *skills* by asking yourself:

- Have I improved my active listening skills so that I continue to learn?

- In what ways am I demonstrating how to ask good questions to prompt others' thinking?

In this activity, you will reflect on your own *values* by asking:

- When I talk about the many values surrounding family, work, and community, what are the ones that rise to the top of importance, and why?

In this activity, you can take *action* by assessing:

- What does it mean to be an ethical communicator in everyday moments?

- How can my communication be a model for others to create a more caring, just world?

The Activity

Complete the chart entitled, *Wrapping It Up*, first individually and then again, in a small group of your classmates. Engaging in collective public discussions generates important, diverse views that all deserve a hearing. During the group discussion, you may find it helpful to share stories that illuminate why something is important to you. You can learn from others why they feel as they do, which can influence your thinking. Of course, context matters so if you and your classmates find yourself generally in similar situations, you will likely find norms or standards that work for all of you. You might even feel strongly that there are guiding, universal principals to which everyone should abide, such as always working for a just decision or always telling the truth no matter the consequences. On the other hand, your group may not all agree on the same ethical principles, yet you will surface the reasons, stories, and discussions that will allow you to understand one another better and come to a group decision. Now that's a noble goal of communication, right?

© Aedka Studio/Shutterstock.com

Wrapping It Up: Summary of Ideas

Individually

As an individual, think about the five most important things you've learned in this class. They don't have to be profound, just important to you. List them here and explain WHY they are important:

Idea/Concept/Term	Why was it important to you?
1.	
2.	
3.	
4.	
5.	

As a Group

As a group, compare your lists and come up with a group list of the five most important things you learned. You should aim for consensus—what does your group think the five most important ideas are? Explain why. Put this chart on your whiteboard, flipchart, or online discussion board.

Idea/Concept/Term	Why was it important to you?
1.	
2.	
3.	
4.	
5.	

Discussion Questions

1. What contributed to making the five concepts you identified the most important to you?

2. Were you surprised at what others identified as their five most important concepts?

3. Did learning what others said cause you to change what you considered the most important learning from the class?

4. What values emerge from having discussions (communicating with others!) about your ethics and others' ethics?

Crafting Your Ethical Voice

Writing a final paper is one way to bring together disparate pieces of learning into a cohesive statement. This is a paper about you, what you think lies ahead for you, and how communication ethics can help you make good decisions in communicating.

In this activity, you will increase your *knowledge* by considering:

- What is the story I can tell here drawing from lived experience, readings, and talking with others?
- How can I write in ways that engage the reader?

In this activity, you will learn *skills* by asking yourself:

- What practices will allow me to write fully, often, and in ways free of distractions?
- What is significant in the story that I can weave throughout my paper?

In this activity, you will reflect on your own *values* by asking:

- Is there a theme around which my values pivot?
- What rich or thick description can I use to make my values come alive in my writing?

In this activity, you can take *action* by assessing:

- How authentic is my paper in reflecting on the actions I will likely take in the future?
- In what ways can I enact my responsibilities now, even prior to future events?

The Activity

While nobody is born a great writer (Goodall, 2000), the more you invest yourself in thinking about what's important, shaping ideas into words, and then giving yourself enough time to make revisions, the better your writing will generally be. In fact, you can even consider writing a dialogic experience if you share drafts of your writing with others. Since you've had so many good discussions with others about communication ethics, we imagine you have a number of peers who could provide important feedback. Now that's something to think about and even try—get feedback on your writing draft from someone in your class.

For this paper, you can organize your ideas in the following way to construct a story of your life and your anticipated communication goals.

- **Introduction and Ethical Situation:** Provide a clear description of a situation you are likely to encounter in your future. You want to think about how communication ethics can provide a roadmap for your responses and responsibilities. If you have a sibling with disabilities that may require your support in the future, that is something to think and write about. Or, maybe you plan to move to a new city upon graduation, away from your family. What does that mean for how you communicate? Will you be the one expected to travel if you want to see family members? If someone you work with or live with falls ill, what responsibilities will you carry? Whether you choose a family, intimate relationship, workplace, or community context, think about what situations you're likely to encounter in the future, pick one, and write about that.

- **Ethical Ideals**: How will you live your life in ways that you communicate ethically, based on what you have learned? Include a discussion of at least three ethical perspectives relevant to your situation, identifying the concrete values embedded in those perspectives.

- **Practical Ethics**: What actions are called for on your part to ensure your values are expressed ethically? In other words, how will you put theory into action in response to your particular situation?

- **References**: Incorporate the required number of readings per your instructor's instructions (this book is one; others may include journal articles, book chapters, websites, etc.) into your final paper, cited according to APA 7th edition and provide full references at the end of your paper.

Tips for Organizing Your Paper:

1. Your paper should be clearly organized, avoid redundancies, and be well written. It should be free of grammatical and spelling errors and written with college-level proficiency.

2. Use a dialogic tone, one that is constructive not judgmental.

3. Focus on ethical communication. For example, to discuss disability rights, your paper should focus on how we talk about people with disabilities and their rights, the controversy surrounding how we decide the extent of accommodations, etc.

4. Be thoughtful as you write and be open to the unexpected to emerge.

5. Share personal experiences, as relevant.

Reference

Goodall, H. L. (2000). *The new ethnography.* AltaMira Press.

Additional Resources

Lamott, A. (1994). *Bird by bird: Some instructions on writing and life.* Pantheon Books.
Poulos, C. (2008). Accidental dialogue: The search for dialogic moments in everyday life. *Communication Theory, 18*(1), 117--138. https://doi.org/10.1111/j.1468-2885.2007.00316.x

Your Ethical Credo

Putting Principles into Practice

At the beginning of this book, you learned about the National Communication Association Ethical Credo. You likely completed the activity, as well, *Developing a Classroom Code of Ethics* or credo. Individuals have also explained what they believe and practice in many settings on a radio show entitled *This I Believe*, which ran on National Public Radio (NPR, n.d.) for 4 years, now has its own website, and started in the 1950s (About this I believe, 2020). The book from the NPR series provides insights into the principles that many people live their lives by (Allison & Gediman, 2007). Now, it's time for you to do the same for your life!

This paper will be written in two parts. In part one, you will write your statement of rights and responsibilities. When you revise your paper for part two, you will incorporate the feedback you receive into your writing as well as your knowledge and experience of communication ethics.

In this activity, you will increase your *knowledge* by considering:

- What communication-based activities or situations are ones in which ethical questions arise?

- If your course is examining social media, consider this question: In what ways is social media advancing that raises new ethical communication concerns?

In this activity, you will learn *skills* by asking yourself:

- How can research activity advance my knowledge to a new level?

- How can I craft an argument to best justify my views?

In this activity, you will reflect on your own *values* by asking:

- How can I affect the quality of my communication and relationships through my ethical communication?

- How can my values be shown in my interpersonal relationships, in my communication in my organization, in my communication in my community, and on social media?

In this activity, you can take *action* by assessing:

- How workable is my ethical credo?

The Activity

This is a research paper, but one probably different from most research papers you've ever written. The goal of this paper is for you to develop your own personal statement on what you think people's rights and responsibilities are when communicating in a networked world.

You will note each right or responsibility and then you will (1) provide a rationale for including it, (2) explain it in relation to at least three terms from this book, (3) relate each portion of your statement to specific experiences working on your class group project or individual reflections, (4) provide, at a minimum, four scholarly references for your statement (four for the whole project), and (5) reflect on how your real-life experiences relate to the rights and responsibility statement you've written.

Think carefully about what you believe and provide thoughtful support for why you believe it. Base your ideas on real-life experiences and not untested ideals. Ethics is the ground where theory and reality meet—where the rubber hits the road.

© iQoncept/Shutterstock.com

Part I: Individual Reflection and Research Paper

Provide your rights and responsibilities' statement:

- Include at least five different statements of rights and responsibilities.

- Present your key ideas about people's rights and responsibilities when communicating in a networked world.

- These should be well-thought-out, carefully considered ideas that you can apply in your everyday life.

Define communication ethics in the context discussed in your class, whether it be interpersonal, organizational, community-based, or on social media:

- Come up with well-justified definitions of your terms, including a discussion of why it's important to understand communication ethics in today's society. You should refer to terms and perspectives from the class for this section.

For your statement, include each of the following:

- Rationale: A clear, logical rationale for the portion of the statement of rights and responsibilities.

- Terms: At least three terms from the readings explained in your statement (though you may want to include more as you'll eventually need 15 terms—see Part II). Please **bold** the terms that you use to make them easier to find.

- References: Cite your sources according to your instructor's guidelines.

Part II: Revising Your Writing and Adding More
Revise your rights and responsibilities statement, your definition of communication ethics in a networked world, and each portion of your statement of rights and responsibilities with its rationale.

- Incorporate new knowledge from additional readings and feedback to each of the above sections of your paper.

Add three terms for each of the five statements of rights and responsibilities (for a new total of 15).

- Please **bold** the terms that you are using to make them easier to find.

Add experiences and examples.

- Relate each portion of your statement to specific experiences of your own or working with others.

Reflect on your experience by responding to the following questions.

- What are the most important ideas you learned from this project?
- What did you gain personally from this experience?
- What did you learn about how real life relates to communication ethics in a networked world? Provide *specific examples.*

Tips for Organization and Writing Style

- Your paper should be clearly organized, and avoid redundancy.
- You should use a professional writing style, which includes proper grammar, spelling, and punctuation.
- In Part II, revise your research paper based on the feedback you received on the first part to receive the most possible points.

References

About This I believe. (2020). www.thisibelieve.org/about/

Allison, J., & Gediman, D. (Eds.). (2007). *This I believe: The personal philosophies of remarkable men and women.* Holt, Henry, & Company, Inc.

NPR. (n.d.). Celebrating four years of 'This I Believe.' Special Series: This I Believe. https://www.npr.org/series/4538138/this-i-believe

Why Communication Ethics is an Important Course

There are many courses you will take throughout your academic journey. The authors of this book believe that a course in communication ethics is essential in a communication curriculum (Ballard et al., 2014; Swenson Lepper et al., 2015) and in any other field of study you are pursuing (Ballard et al., 2016). As stated in the beginning of this text, our goal is to help you unpack, discover, and recognize the importance of becoming an ethical communicator in a diverse world. As you finish this course, we hope you encourage others to take a class in communication ethics and that you walk away from this course realizing the "pragmatic" nature of communication ethics (Arnett et al., 2018, p. xii).

In this activity, you will increase your *knowledge* by considering:

- What communication ethics ideas are essential to discuss with first-year students?

- What persuasive techniques can be used to convince students to take a course in communication ethics?

In this activity, you will learn *skills,* by asking yourself:

- How can you speak in ways that inform and persuade students about communication ethics?

- How can you engage an audience that might never have heard of communication ethics?

In this activity, you will reflect on your own *values* by asking yourself:

- What ideas or concepts resonated with you throughout the semester?

- What examples from your life can offer clarity when explaining communication ethics?

In this activity, you can take *action* by assessing:

- What have you learned in this course that can be applied to everyday interaction with others?

- How has your communication changed after this course?

The Activity

Imagine you are a guest speaker addressing incoming first-year students at your university. Your assignment is to explain the importance of communication ethics in a diverse world in such a way that new students find your presentation one that is understandable, holds interest, and encourages them to take a course in communication ethics.

- The **introduction** should include an attention grabber and thesis statement.

- The **body** of the presentation should integrate at least three big ideas and three ethical perspectives from class supported by examples from your life.

- Your **conclusion** needs to restate your purpose and provide a call to action to take a course in communication ethics.

- The recommended time is 5-7 minutes.

References

Arnett, R. C., Fritz, J. H., & Bell McManus, L. M. (2018). *Communication ethics: Dialogue and difference* (2nd ed.). Kendall Hunt.

Ballard, R. L., Hoffer (Vélez Ortiz), M., & Bell McManus, L. M. (2016). Communication ethics: A vital resource in an ever-changing world. *Choice: Current Reviews for Academic Libraries, 54,* 155–164.

Ballard, R. L., Bell McManus, L. M., Holba, A. M., Jovanovic, S., Tompkins, P. S., Charron, L. J. N., Hoffer (Vélez Ortiz), M. L., Leavitt, M. A. & Swenson-Lepper, T. (2014). Teaching communication ethics as central to the discipline. *Journal of the Association for Communication Administration, 33*(2), 2–20.

Swenson-Lepper, T., Leavitt, M. A., Hoffer (Vélez Ortiz), M., Charron, L. N., Ballard, R. L., Bell McManus, L. M., Holba, A. M., Jovanovic, S. & Tompkins, P. S. (2015). Communication ethics in the communication curriculum: United States, Canada, and Puerto Rico. *Communication Education, 64*(4). 472–490.